Collins

Key Stage 3
Biblical Literacy

Robert Orme
Series Editor: Robert Orme

William Collins' dream of knowledge for all began with the publication of his first book in 1819. A self-educated mill worker, he not only enriched millions of lives, but also founded a flourishing publishing house. Today, staying true to this spirit, Collins books are packed with inspiration, innovation and practical expertise. They place you at the centre of a world of possibility and give you exactly what you need to explore it.

Collins. Freedom to teach

Published by Collins
An imprint of HarperCollins*Publishers*
The News Building
1 London Bridge Street
London SE1 9GF

10 9 8 7 6 5 4 3 2 1

ISBN 978-0-00-822767-8

A catalogue record for this book is available from the British Library

Publisher: Joanna Ramsay
Editor: Hannah Dove
Author: Robert Orme
Series Editor: Robert Orme
Development Editor: Sonya Newland
Project Manager: Emily Hooton
Copy-editor: Jill Morris
Image researcher: Shelley Noronha
Proof-reader: Nikky Twyman
Cover designer: We Are Laura
Cover image: ASP Religion/Alamy
Production controller: Rachel Weaver
Typesetter: QBS
Printed and bound by CPI Group (UK) Ltd, Croydon, CR0 4YY

Contents

Introduction

Every day, millions of people all over the world pick up and read the Bible. However, not only is the Bible one of the most popular books ever printed – it is one of the most controversial. In some countries, leaders have banned people from reading it. In other parts of the world, the Bible is considered so important that is shapes the laws that people must follow.

The Bible is the most significant text for followers of the world's largest religion, Christianity. The books in the first section of the Bible are also important to followers of Judaism, who include them in their scriptures. Knowing about the Bible will help you understand more about the origins, beliefs and practices of these two religions.

Although the Bible is often referred to as a book, in fact it is a collection of texts by many different people writing at different times. The first part of the Christian Bible is known as the Old Testament and the second part the New Testament. Between them, they contain many stories. Some tell of murder, betrayal, lies and scandal; others are about love, bravery, sacrifice and miracles. As you read them, you will discover some extraordinary ideas and learn about remarkable individuals who have inspired some of the most famous art, music and literature ever created, and who continue to inspire millions of people around the globe.

Robert Orme (Series Editor)

Concise topic introductions set the scene and focus your learning.

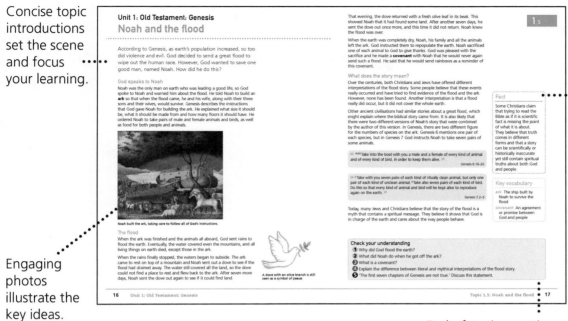

Engaging photos illustrate the key ideas.

Fact boxes provide bite-sized details.

End-of-topic questions are designed to check and consolidate your understanding.

Key fact boxes help you to revise and remember the main points from each unit.

Key vocabulary lists for each unit help you define and remember important terms.

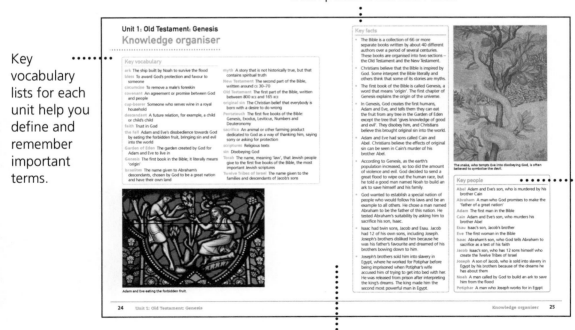

Key people boxes summarise the key figures of the time.

Knowledge organisers can be used to revise and quiz yourself on key dates, definitions and descriptions.

Old Testament: Genesis

In the first section of this book, you will explore some of the most famous and influential stories found in the first book of the Bible – Genesis. You will examine what it says about the creation of the world and also the first humans – Adam and Eve. You will see how they disobey God and discover why one of their sons becomes the first of many murderers in the Bible. You will also examine why God decides to flood the earth, why he tells a man called Abraham to kill his son and how he looks after a man named Joseph, who finds himself imprisoned in a foreign land as a result of jealousy and lies.

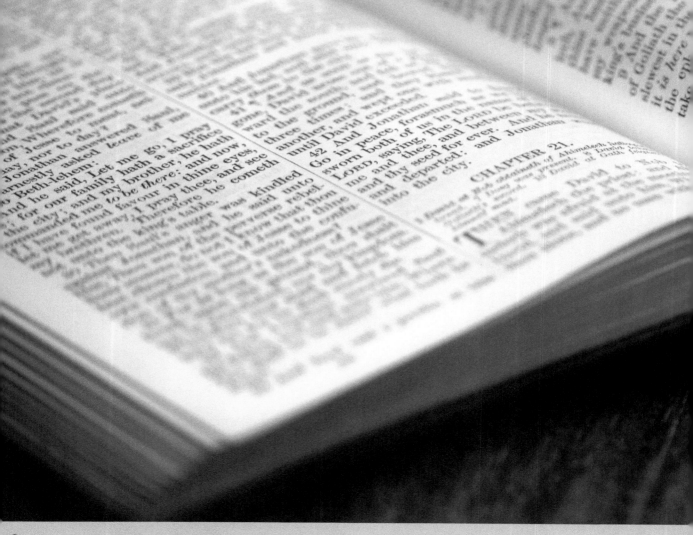

Unit 1: Old Testament: Genesis
What is the Bible?

What is in the Bible and when was it written?

The world's bestseller

No book ever written has been reprinted as many times as the Bible. It has been translated into more than 550 languages and is read by millions of people all over the world every day. At times over the past few hundred years, the Bible has been banned in some countries, and even today there are places where it is illegal to have a copy.

The Bible.

One book or many books?

The word 'Bible' comes from the Greek word *biblia*, which means 'books'. This is fitting, as the Bible is not a single book but a collection of 66 or more separate books written by about 40 different authors over a period of several centuries. These books are organised into two sections – the **Old Testament** and the **New Testament**. They contain different types of writing. For example, there are stories, history, laws, visions, poems, songs and letters. Each book in the Bible is divided into chapters and verses.

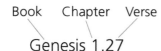

Book   Chapter   Verse

Genesis 1.27

Shakespeare and the Bible

William Shakespeare refers to the Bible more than 1200 times in his plays. He makes reference to 18 books in the Old Testament and 18 in the New Testament. There are so many references to the opening chapters of Genesis (the first book in the Bible) that some experts think that Shakespeare probably knew these by heart.

The Old Testament

Most biblical scholars think that the Old Testament was written between 800 BCE and 165 BCE. The first five books in the Bible are sometimes collectively referred to as the **Pentateuch**. The first book of the Pentateuch is **Genesis** – a word that means 'origin'. The first chapter of Genesis explains the origins of the universe.

After describing how God creates the universe, Genesis tells how he puts two people – Adam and Eve – on earth. As the world becomes populated,

The Tanakh

Jewish **scriptures** contain many books that are also in the Old Testament of the Bible, although they appear in a different order. Jewish scriptures are called the Tanakh and the first five books of this are the same as those in the Bible. Jews call these five books the **Torah**, which means 'law'. Remember, the New Testament is *not* part of Jewish scripture.

The Torah forms the first part of the Jewish scriptures, which are sometimes called the Hebrew Bible as they were written in this language.

God chooses a particular nation of people, the **Israelites**, to follow and obey him. The Old Testament describes how the Israelites try to honour God. It is filled with stories about violence, love, murder and corrupt rulers.

The New Testament

The first four books of the New Testament describe the life and death of a man called Jesus, who lived about 2000 years ago. Acts, the fifth book of the New Testament, explains how the religion of Christianity grew from Judaism after Jesus's death. The rest of the New Testament is made up of letters written to the early Christians, giving them guidance on what to believe and how they should live their lives.

The importance of the Bible

The Bible is extremely important to Christians. They believe that it is inspired by God, so it forms the basis of many church services, prayers and songs. Many Christians also study the Bible at home to learn more about God and how he wants them to live.

As with any text written so long ago, we cannot know for sure whether the events in the Bible were recorded accurately, or if they really took place at all. Different groups of Christians have different opinions on this issue, as you will see. An atheist might say that much of the Bible cannot be accurate, because God does not exist or because many of the stories in it could not possibly have happened. Others might argue that the authors were trying to persuade people to follow their beliefs, which makes their writings unreliable.

Translations of the Bible

There are many versions of the Bible. Different groups of Christians include different books in their Bible. For example, Protestants have 66 books in their Bible – 39 in the Old Testament and 27 in the New Testament. Catholics include 7 more books in their Old Testament, so there are 73 books in total in their Bible.

The Old Testament was originally written in Hebrew, while the New Testament was written in Greek. Over time, the Bible has been translated into different languages. However, even within the English language, there are many different translations. Some translations aim to translate every word in English as precisely as possible. Others focus on translating the message rather than the exact words. The Bible passages in this book are taken from the Good News translation, which is popular amongst Christians.

Key vocabulary

Genesis The first book in the Bible; it literally means 'origin'

Israelites The name given to Abraham's descendants, chosen by God to be a great nation and have their own land

New Testament The second part of the Bible, written around CE 30–70

Old Testament The first part of the Bible, written between 800 BCE and 165 BCE

Pentateuch The first five books of the Bible: Genesis, Exodus, Leviticus, Numbers and Deuteronomy

scriptures Religious texts

Torah The name, meaning 'law', that Jewish people give to the first five books of the Bible, the most important Jewish scriptures

Check your understanding

1. What are the two different sections of the Bible called?
2. Why might someone say that the Bible is like a library?
3. What is the difference between the Tanakh and the Old Testament?
4. Why is the Bible important to Christians?
5. Why might an atheist think that much of the Bible cannot be true?

Unit 1: Old Testament: Genesis
Creation

How do Christians interpret the story of creation at the start of Genesis?

A painting by Michelangelo showing God creating Adam.

1 ❝ ¹In the beginning, when God created the universe, ²the earth was formless and desolate. The raging ocean that covered everything was engulfed in total darkness, and the Spirit of God was moving over the water. ³Then God commanded, 'Let there be light' – and light appeared. ⁴God was pleased with what he saw. Then he separated the light from the darkness, ⁵and he named the light 'Day' and the darkness 'Night'. Evening passed and morning came – that was the first day. ❞

❝ ⁶⁻⁷Then God commanded, 'Let there be a dome to divide the water and to keep it in two separate places' – and it was done. So God made a dome, and it separated the water under it from the water above it. ⁸He named the dome 'Sky'. Evening passed and morning came – that was the second day. ❞

❝ ⁹Then God commanded, 'Let the water below the sky come together in one place, so that the land will appear' – and it was done. ¹⁰He named the land 'Earth', and the water which had come together he named 'Sea'. And God was pleased with what he saw. ¹¹Then he commanded, 'Let the earth produce all kinds of plants, those that bear grain and those that bear fruit' – and it was done. ¹²So the earth produced all kinds of plants, and God was pleased with what he saw. ¹³Evening passed and morning came – that was the third day. ❞

❝ ¹⁴Then God commanded, 'Let lights appear in the sky to separate day from night and to show the time when days, years, and religious festivals begin; ¹⁵they will shine in the sky to give light to the earth' – and it was done. ¹⁶So God made the two larger lights, the sun to rule over the day and the moon to rule over the night; he also made the stars. ¹⁷He placed the lights in the sky to shine on the earth, ¹⁸to rule over the day and the night, and to separate light from darkness. And God was pleased with what he saw. ¹⁹Evening passed and morning came – that was the fourth day. ❞

❝ ²⁰Then God commanded, 'Let the water be filled with many kinds of living beings, and let the air be filled with birds.' ²¹So God created the great sea monsters, all kinds of creatures that live in the water, and all kinds of birds. And God was pleased with what he saw. ²²He blessed them all and told the creatures that live in the water to reproduce, and to fill the sea, and he told the birds to increase in number. ²³Evening passed and morning came – that was the fifth day. ❞

66 24 Then God commanded, 'Let the earth produce all kinds of animal life: domestic and wild, large and small' – and it was done. 25 So God made them all, and he was pleased with what he saw. 99

66 26 Then God said, 'And now we will make human beings; they will be like us and resemble us. They will have power over the fish, the birds, and all animals, domestic and wild, large and small.' 27 So God created human beings, making them to be like himself. He created them male and female, 28 blessed them, and said, 'Have many children, so that your descendants will live all over the earth and bring it under their control. I am putting you in charge of the fish, the birds, and all the wild animals. 29 I have provided all kinds of grain and all kinds of fruit for you to eat; 30 but for all the wild animals and for all the birds I have provided grass and leafy plants for food' – and it was done. 31 God looked at everything he had made, and he was very pleased. Evening passed and morning came – that was the sixth day. 99

66 1 And so the whole universe was completed. 2 By the seventh day God finished what he had been doing and stopped working. 3 He blessed the seventh day and set it apart as a special day, because by that day he had completed his creation and stopped working. 4 And that is how the universe was created. 99

Genesis 1.1–2.4

Literal interpretations of the Bible

Some Christians interpret the Bible literally, claiming that it describes a series of real events. Because they believe that the world was created exactly as described in Genesis, these Christians disagree with scientists about the origins of the universe. In the seventeenth century, a man named James Ussher looked at all the dates in the Bible to try and work out the earth's age. He came to the conclusion that it was 6000 years old. However, scientists today believe the earth is thousands of millions of years old.

Liberal interpretations of the Bible

Not everyone interprets the Bible literally. Many Christians think that some stories in it are **myths** – they are not factually accurate, but contain spiritual lessons or truths that we can learn from. According to this liberal interpretation, the creation story in Genesis is not a factual description of how and when God made everything. It is just trying to teach that God is the powerful creator of all things.

JACOBUS USSERIUS, ARCHIEPISCOPUS, ARMACHANUS, TOTIUS HIBERNIÆ PRIMAS

Archbishop James Ussher dated the creation of the universe to 22 October 4004 BCE.

Key vocabulary

myth A story that is not historically true, but which contains spiritual truth

---

Check your understanding

1 According to Genesis, what happened on each day of creation?

2 Why might someone say the creation story shows that humans are important?

3 What is meant by 'interpretation'?

4 Explain the difference between a literal and liberal interpretation of the creation story.

5 What might Genesis chapter 1 teach a Christian about the nature of God?

Unit 1: Old Testament: Genesis
The Fall

God told Adam and Eve they could eat the fruit from any tree in the **Garden of Eden** except the tree that 'gives knowledge of good and evil'. Why did they disobey him?

This stained-glass window shows Eve tempting Adam with the apple.

3 66 ¹ Now the snake was the most cunning animal that the Lord God had made. The snake asked the woman, 'Did God really tell you not to eat fruit from any tree in the garden?' 99

66 ² 'We may eat the fruit of any tree in the garden,' the woman answered, ³ 'except the tree in the middle of it. God told us not to eat the fruit of that tree or even touch it; if we do, we will die.' 99

66 ⁴ The snake replied, 'That's not true; you will not die. ⁵ God said that because he knows that when you eat it, you will be like God and know what is good and what is bad.' 99

66 ⁶ The woman saw how beautiful the tree was and how good its fruit would be to eat, and she thought how wonderful it would be to become wise. So she took some of the fruit and ate it. Then she gave some to her husband, and he also ate it. ⁷ As soon as they had eaten it, they were given understanding and realised that they were naked; so they sewed fig leaves together and covered themselves. 99

66 ⁸ That evening they heard the Lord God walking in the garden, and they hid from him among the trees. ⁹ But the Lord God called out to the man, 'Where are you?' 99

66 ¹⁰ He answered, 'I heard you in the garden; I was afraid and hid from you, because I was naked.' 99

> [11] 'Who told you that you were naked?' God asked. 'Did you eat the fruit that I told you not to eat?'

> [12] The man answered, 'The woman you put here with me gave me the fruit, and I ate it.'

> [13] The Lord God asked the woman, 'Why did you do this?' She replied, 'The snake tricked me into eating it.'

God pronounces judgement

> [14] Then the Lord God said to the snake, 'You will be punished for this; you alone of all the animals must bear this curse: from now on you will crawl on your belly, and you will have to eat dust as long as you live. [15] I will make you and the woman hate each other; her offspring and yours will always be enemies. Her offspring will crush your head, and you will bite her offspring's heel.'

> [16] And he said to the woman, 'I will increase your trouble in pregnancy and your pain in giving birth. In spite of this, you will still have desire for your husband, yet you will be subject to him.'

> [17] And he said to the man, 'You listened to your wife and ate the fruit which I told you not to eat. Because of what you have done, the ground will be under a curse. You will have to work hard all your life to make it produce enough food for you. [18] It will produce weeds and thorns, and you will have to eat wild plants. [19] You will have to work hard and sweat to make the soil produce anything, until you go back to the soil from which you were formed. You were made from soil, and you will become soil again.'

> [20] Adam named his wife Eve, because she was the mother of all human beings. [21] And the Lord God made clothes out of animal skins for Adam and his wife, and he clothed them.

Genesis 3.1–21

The snake, who tempts Eve into disobeying God, is often believed to symbolise the devil.

Adam and Eve's sin

At first, Adam and Eve lived happily in the Garden of Eden in a perfect relationship with each other and with God. There was no evil or suffering. However, after they disobeyed God, he made them leave the Garden of Eden and life became difficult for them.

The story of the **Fall** is very important to Christians. Those who interpret it literally believe that **sin**, evil and suffering entered the world as a result of Adam and Eve's actions. Other Christians believe that the story is a myth designed to teach us how humans instinctively want to disobey God and to show how our relationship with God is damaged by this disobedience. Whether Christians interpret the Fall literally or not, most agree that the story teaches that every human is born with a desire to ignore God and do wrong. This is known as **original sin**.

Key vocabulary

Fall Adam and Eve's disobedience towards God by eating the forbidden fruit, bringing sin and evil into the world

Garden of Eden The garden created by God for Adam and Eve to live in

original sin The Christian belief that everybody is born with a desire to do wrong

sin Disobeying God

Check your understanding

1. How did Adam and Eve disobey God?
2. What were the consequences of Adam and Eve's actions?
3. What is meant by 'original sin'?
4. What characteristics do Adam and Eve show in the story (for example, jealousy, shame)?
5. What meaning might the story of the Fall have for a Christian interpreting it as a myth?

Unit 1: Old Testament: Genesis
Cain and Abel

The first of many murders in the Bible is committed by Adam and Eve's son Cain, who kills his brother Abel. What caused his fit of jealousy and rage?

After Adam and Eve were sent out of the Garden of Eden, they had two sons: Cain and Abel. Cain was a farmer and Abel was a shepherd. One day, both boys decided to offer a **sacrifice** to God. This may have been to show respect, to give thanks for good things or to gain God's protection from danger.

Abel making his sacrifice to God.

66 3 After some time, Cain brought some of his harvest and gave it as an offering to the Lord. 4 Then Abel brought the first lamb born to one of his sheep, killed it, and gave the best parts of it as an offering. The Lord was pleased with Abel and his offering, 5 but he rejected Cain and his offering. Cain became furious, and he scowled in anger. 6 Then the Lord said to Cain, 'Why are you angry? Why that scowl on your face? 7 If you had done the right thing, you would be smiling; but because you have done evil, sin is crouching at your door. It wants to rule you, but you must overcome it.' 99

66 8 Then Cain said to his brother Abel, 'Let's go out in the fields.' When they were out in the fields, Cain turned on his brother and killed him. 99

66 9 The Lord asked Cain, 'Where is your brother Abel?' 99

66 He answered, 'I don't know. Am I supposed to take care of my brother?' 10 Then the Lord said, 'Why have you done this terrible thing? Your brother's blood is crying out to me from the ground, like a voice calling for revenge. 11 You are placed under a curse and can no longer farm the soil. It has soaked up your brother's blood as if it had opened its mouth to receive it when you killed him. 12 If you try to grow crops, the soil will not produce anything; you will be a homeless wanderer on the earth.' 99

66 13 And Cain said to the Lord, 'This punishment is too hard for me to bear. 14 You are driving me off the land and away from your presence. I will be a homeless wanderer on the earth, and anyone who finds me will kill me.' 99

66 15 But the Lord answered, 'No. If anyone kills you, seven lives will be taken in revenge.' So the Lord put a mark on Cain to warn anyone who met him not to kill him. 16 And Cain went away from the Lord's presence and lived in a land called 'Wandering', which is east of Eden. 99

Genesis 4.3–16

Echoes of Eden

Many Christians believe that, since Adam and Eve's first act of disobedience, humans have acted on their desire to commit sin. This can be seen in how Cain behaves after God refuses to accept his sacrifice. Although God warned Cain to overcome his anger, Cain did not listen. The combination of his anger and jealousy towards his brother ended in murder.

Just as God had sent Adam and Eve away from paradise, he also punished Cain by sending him out into the wild, away from the safety of his family's farm. Cain was afraid of what travelling tribes might do to him out in the wilderness, but God 'marked' him. Biblical scholars are unsure what form this mark might have taken, but it was a sign to potential attackers that Cain was protected by God, so they would leave him alone.

Genesis does not explain why God rejected Cain's sacrifice. It might have been because Abel offered his finest crops, but Cain did not make as much effort to give God the best possible sacrifice. However, the text does not say this. Many Christians believe that the reason Cain's sacrifice was rejected was because Abel offered his with faith, whereas Cain did so without faith, thoughtlessly, as if it did not mean much to him.

After murdering his brother, Cain was banished to the wilderness.

Fact

The people in the early chapters of Genesis lived for a very long time. When Adam and Eve are 130 years old, they have another son, named Seth. Adam lives another 800 years after this and Seth lives for a total of 912 years. However, these numbers are usually believed to be symbolic, not literal!

Key vocabulary

sacrifice An animal or foodstuff dedicated to God as a way of thanking him, saying sorry or asking for protection

Check your understanding

1. Why did people in the Old Testament make offerings to God?
2. What did Abel sacrifice to God?
3. What happened after Cain's sacrifice was rejected?
4. What might this story teach Christians about the nature of God?
5. Why might a Christian say this story has similarities with the story of the Fall?

Unit 1: Old Testament: Genesis
Noah and the flood

According to Genesis, as earth's population increased, so too did violence and evil. God decided to send a great flood to wipe out the human race. However, God wanted to save one good man, named Noah. How did he do this?

God speaks to Noah

Noah was the only man on earth who was leading a good life, so God spoke to Noah and warned him about the flood. He told Noah to build an **ark** so that when the flood came, he and his wife, along with their three sons and their wives, would survive. Genesis describes the instructions that God gave Noah for building the ark. He explained what size it should be, what it should be made from and how many floors it should have. He ordered Noah to take pairs of male and female animals and birds, as well as food for both people and animals.

Noah built the ark, taking care to follow all of God's instructions.

The flood

When the ark was finished and the animals all aboard, God sent rains to flood the earth. Eventually, the water covered even the mountains, and all living things on earth died, except those in the ark.

When the rains finally stopped, the waters began to subside. The ark came to rest on top of a mountain and Noah sent out a dove to see if the flood had drained away. The water still covered all the land, so the dove could not find a place to rest and flew back to the ark. After seven more days, Noah sent the dove out again to see if it could find land.

A dove with an olive branch is still seen as a symbol of peace.

That evening, the dove returned with a fresh olive leaf in its beak. This showed Noah that it had found some land. After another seven days, he sent the dove out once more, and this time it did not return. Noah knew the flood was over.

When the earth was completely dry, Noah, his family and all the animals left the ark. God instructed them to repopulate the earth. Noah sacrificed one of each animal to God to give thanks. God was pleased with the sacrifice and he made a **covenant** with Noah that he would never again send such a flood. He said that he would send rainbows as a reminder of this covenant.

What does the story mean?

Over the centuries, both Christians and Jews have offered different interpretations of the flood story. Some people believe that these events really occurred and have tried to find evidence of the flood and the ark. However, none has been found. Another interpretation is that a flood really did occur, but it did not cover the whole earth.

Other ancient civilisations had similar stories about a great flood, which might explain where the biblical story came from. It is also likely that there were two different versions of Noah's story that were combined by the author of this version. In Genesis, there are two different figure for the numbers of species on the ark. Genesis 6 mentions one pair of each species, but in Genesis 7 God instructs Noah to take seven pairs of some animals.

> 66 19-20 Take into the boat with you a male and a female of every kind of animal and of every kind of bird, in order to keep them alive. 99
>
> Genesis 6.19–20

> 66 2 Take with you seven pairs of each kind of ritually clean animal, but only one pair of each kind of unclean animal. 3 Take also seven pairs of each kind of bird. Do this so that every kind of animal and bird will be kept alive to reproduce again on the earth. 99
>
> Genesis 7.2–3

Today, many Jews and Christians believe that the story of the flood is a myth that contains a spiritual message. They believe it shows that God is in charge of the earth and cares about the way people behave.

Fact

Some Christians claim that trying to read the Bible as if it is scientific fact is missing the point of what it is about. They believe that truth comes in different forms and that a story can be scientifically or historically inaccurate yet still contain spiritual truths about both God and people.

Key vocabulary

ark The ship built by Noah to survive the flood

covenant An agreement or promise between God and people

Check your understanding

1 Why did God flood the earth?

2 What did Noah do when he got off the ark?

3 What is a covenant?

4 Explain the difference between literal and mythical interpretations of the flood story.

5 'The first seven chapters of Genesis are not true.' Discuss this statement.

Unit 1: Old Testament: Genesis
Abraham and Isaac

God wanted to establish a nation of people who would follow his laws and be an example to all others. How did God test Abraham to see if he was the right man to be the father of this nation?

22 **1** Some time later God tested Abraham; he called to him, 'Abraham!' And Abraham answered, 'Yes, here I am!'

2 'Take your son,' God said, 'your only son, Isaac, whom you love so much, and go to the land of Moriah. There on a mountain that I will show you, offer him as a sacrifice to me.'

3 Early the next morning Abraham cut some wood for the sacrifice, loaded his donkey, and took Isaac and two servants with him. They started out for the place that God had told him about. **4** On the third day Abraham saw the place in the distance. **5** Then he said to the servants, 'Stay here with the donkey. The boy and I will go over there and worship, and then we will come back to you.'

6 Abraham made Isaac carry the wood for the sacrifice, and he himself carried a knife and live coals for starting the fire. As they walked along together, **7** Isaac spoke up, 'Father!'

He answered, 'Yes, my son?'

Isaac asked, 'I see that you have the coals and the wood, but where is the lamb for the sacrifice?'

8 Abraham answered, 'God himself will provide one.' And the two of them walked on together.

9 When they came to the place which God had told him about, Abraham built an altar and arranged the wood on it. He tied up his son and placed him on the altar, on top of the wood.

10 Then he picked up the knife to kill him. **11** But the angel of the Lord called to him from heaven, 'Abraham, Abraham!'

He answered, 'Yes, here I am.'

12 'Don't hurt the boy or do anything to him,' he said. 'Now I know that you honour and obey God, because you have not kept back your only son from him.'

13 Abraham looked around and saw a ram caught in a bush by its horns. He went and got it and offered it as a burnt offering instead of his son. **14** Abraham named that place 'The Lord Provides'. And even today people say, 'On the Lord's mountain he provides.'

15 The angel of the Lord called to Abraham from heaven a second time, **16** 'I make a vow by my own name – the Lord is speaking – that I will richly bless you. Because you did this and did not keep back your only son from me, **17** I promise that I will give you as many **descendants** as there are stars in the sky or grains of sand along the seashore. Your descendants will conquer their enemies. **18** All the nations will ask me to bless them as I have blessed your descendants – all because you obeyed my command.'

Genesis 22.1–18

The test of Abraham

To make sure that Abraham was the right man to lead his chosen people, God decided to test his **faith**. Chapter 22 of Genesis describes how God asks Abraham to sacrifice his son, Isaac. In ancient times, people may have killed their firstborn sons as an offering to their gods, but this would have been a particularly great sacrifice for Abraham. It had taken many years for he and his wife Sarah to conceive a child, and according to Genesis Abraham was 100 years old when Isaac was born. It was an act of great faith to trust God enough to kill his child.

By being willing to sacrifice Isaac, Abraham passed God's test. God made a covenant with Abraham that his descendants would form a great nation, conquer their enemies and populate their own special land. In return, Abraham was told to **circumcise** all the men in his tribe, to mark them out as the chosen worshippers of God.

Isaac carried the wood up the mountain, not realising he was to be the sacrifice.

As Abraham was about to sacrifice Isaac, an angel appeared and stopped him.

The importance of Abraham

Abraham is an important figure in Islam as well as in Judaism and Christianity. These three religions are sometimes called the 'Abrahamic religions'. Their followers see Abraham's faith as a great example. The story of Abraham's sacrifice is also found in the holy book for Muslims, the Qur'an, but it contains some different details – for example, in the Qur'an it is not Isaac whom Abraham is asked to sacrifice, but his other son, Ishmael. Jews believe that the covenant that God made with Abraham still stands and that they are the physical and spiritual descendants of Abraham.

Key vocabulary

circumcise To remove a male's foreskin

descendant A future relation, for example, a child or child's child

faith Trust in God

Check your understanding

1. What did God ask Abraham to do?
2. Why was obeying God's request difficult for Abraham?
3. How did God reward Abraham's faith?
4. Why did God test Abraham? Use the word 'descendants' in your answer.
5. 'It was wrong for God to tell Abraham to kill his son.' Discuss this statement.

Unit 1: Old Testament: Genesis
Jacob and his sons

What did Jacob's sons do when their brother Joseph told them that he dreamed of them bowing down to him?

Jacob and Esau

Isaac had twin sons – Esau and Jacob. The book of Genesis describes how the boys fought even in their mother's womb and continued to battle each other as they grew up.

When Isaac was approaching the end of his life, he decided he wanted to **bless** Esau, the elder of the twins. He told Esau to hunt for some food so that he could bless him over a tasty meal. Jacob heard about this and wanted to receive the blessing instead of Esau. Isaac was old and could not see very well, so Jacob decided to trick his father into thinking that he was Esau.

Jacob knew that if Isaac touched him he would know the difference, because Esau was much hairier than he was. He waited until Esau was out hunting, then wrapped himself in goatskin and went to Isaac to receive the blessing. Isaac was confused – while his son felt like Esau, he sounded like Jacob. However, he gave the blessing anyway.

When Esau returned and found out what had happened, he was furious. Jacob was afraid and ran away into the wilderness. There, God spoke to him in a dream, reminding him of the covenant that he had made with Jacob's grandfather, Abraham. Again, God said that Abraham would have many descendants and that they would have their own land. Jacob married and had 12 sons, each of whom later had his own large family.

Isaac blessing Jacob.

> 66 [12] He dreamt that he saw a stairway reaching from earth to heaven, with angels going up and coming down on it. [13] and there was the Lord standing beside him. 'I am the Lord, the God of Abraham and Isaac,' he said. 'I will give to you and to your descendants this land on which you are lying. [14] they will be as numerous as the specks of dust on the earth. They will extend their territory in all directions, and through you and your descendants I will bless all the nations. [15] remember, I will be with you and protect you wherever you go, and I will bring you back to this land. I will not leave you until I have done all that I have promised you.' 99
>
> Genesis 28.12–15

Joseph the dreamer

Joseph was Jacob's favourite son. Jacob gave him a stunning long-sleeved robe to wear. It would have been difficult for Joseph to work hard looking after his father's sheep and goats while wearing this robe, and he probably was not made to take on all the tasks that his brothers had to do. Jacob's other sons hated Joseph and treated him unkindly. They did not like the fact that he was their father's favourite or that he would often tell tales on them. To make matters worse, Joseph used to tell his brothers that he had dreams about them bowing down to him.

Joseph's brothers showed their father his blood-stained robe to convince him his favourite son had been killed by an animal.

> ❝ 5 One night Joseph had a dream, and when he told his brothers about it, they hated him even more. 6 He said, 'Listen to the dream I had. 7 We were all in the field tying up sheaves of wheat, when my sheaf got up and stood up straight. Yours formed a circle around mine and bowed down to it.' ❞
>
> ❝ 8 'Do you think you are going to be a king and rule over us?' his brothers asked. So they hated him even more because of his dreams and because of what he said about them. ❞
>
> ❝ 9 Then Joseph had another dream and told his brothers, 'I had another dream, in which I saw the sun, the moon, and eleven stars bowing down to me.' ❞
>
> ❝ 10 He also told the dream to his father, and his father scolded him: 'What kind of a dream is that? Do you think that your mother, your brothers, and I are going to come and bow down to you?' 11 Joseph's brothers were jealous of him, but his father kept thinking about the whole matter. ❞
>
> Genesis 37.5–11

Sold into slavery

One day, Joseph's brothers decided that they had had enough of him, so they sold him to the Egyptians as a slave. They took his robe and covered it in goat blood, then took it back to their father so that Jacob would think Joseph was dead. Jacob was devastated. He tore his clothes and declared that he would spend the rest of his life mourning his dead son.

Key vocabulary

bless To award God's protection and favour to someone

Activity

In pairs, place the following eight characters in the order in which they appear in the Bible.

- Abraham
- Eve
- Adam
- Moses
- Noah
- Jacob
- Isaac
- Joseph

Check your understanding

1 What did Isaac want to do before he died?

2 How did Jacob trick Isaac?

3 What did God say to Jacob in his dream?

4 Give three reasons why Joseph's brothers did not like him.

5 Explain what happens in Genesis 37.5–11.

Unit 1: Old Testament: Genesis
Joseph in Egypt

What happened to Joseph in Egypt?

Life in Egypt

When Joseph arrived in Egypt he was sold to a man named Potiphar, who was one of the king's officials. Joseph gained Potiphar's trust and was eventually put in charge of the whole household. Joseph was well-built and handsome and Potiphar's wife was attracted to him. Day after day she tried to persuade Joseph to get into bed with her, but each time he refused to disrespect Potiphar and sin against God by spending time with her.

One day, Potiphar's wife grabbed Joseph by his cloak and tried to make him go to bed with her. Joseph abandoned his cloak and ran out of the house. Potiphar's wife called for all the servants and told them Joseph had tried to get into bed with her and had then run away when she started to scream. When Potiphar heard of this, he was furious, and threw Joseph into prison.

Joseph escaping Potiphar's wife.

Joseph in jail

Joseph's fellow inmates were a baker and a **cup-bearer** who had worked for the king. During their time in prison, these two men had dreams, which they described to Joseph. Joseph told them that God knows the meaning of all dreams and would reveal this meaning to Joseph. He explained that the cup-bearer's dream meant he would be freed from prison, but the baker's dream meant that he would be killed. Joseph's interpretations turned out to be correct.

Two years later, the king began having strange dreams. By this time, the cup-bearer was working for the king again and he told him about Joseph's ability to understand dreams. The king ordered Joseph to be brought to him straight away.

66 14 The king sent for Joseph, and he was immediately brought from the prison. After he had shaved and changed his clothes, he came into the king's presence. 15 The king said to him, 'I have had a dream, and no one can explain it. I have been told that you can interpret dreams.' 99

66 16 Joseph answered, 'I cannot, Your Majesty, but God will give a favourable interpretation.' 99

66 17 The king said, 'I dreamt that I was standing on the bank of the Nile, 18 when seven cows, fat and sleek, came up out of the river and began feeding on the grass. 19 Then seven other cows came up which were thin and bony. They were the poorest cows I have ever seen anywhere in Egypt. 20 The thin cows ate up the fat ones, 21 but no one would have known it, because they looked just as bad as before. Then I woke up. 22 I also dreamt that I saw seven heads of grain which were full and ripe, growing on one stalk. 23 Then seven heads of grain sprouted, thin and scorched by the desert wind, 24 and the thin heads of grain swallowed the full ones. I told the dreams to the magicians, but none of them could explain them to me.' 99

> 25 Joseph said to the king, 'The two dreams mean the same thing; God has told you what he is going to do. 26 The seven fat cows are seven years, and the seven full heads of grain are also seven years; they have the same meaning. 27 The seven thin cows which came up later and the seven thin heads of grain scorched by the desert wind are seven years of famine. 28 It is just as I told you – God has shown you what he is going to do. 29 There will be seven years of great plenty in all the land of Egypt. 30 After that, there will be seven years of famine, and all the good years will be forgotten, because the famine will ruin the country. 31 The time of plenty will be entirely forgotten, because the famine which follows will be so terrible. 32 The repetition of your dream means that the matter is fixed by God and that he will make it happen in the near future. 99

> 33 'Now you should choose some man with wisdom and insight and put him in charge of the country. 34 You must also appoint other officials and take a fifth of the crops during the seven years of plenty. 35 Order them to collect all the food during the good years that are coming, and give them authority to store up grain in the cities and guard it. 99

> 36 'The food will be a reserve supply for the country during the seven years of famine which are going to come on Egypt. In this way the people will not starve.' 99

Genesis 41.14–36

Through Joseph, God explained what the king's dreams about the cows and the corn meant.

Joseph's brothers travel to Egypt

The king followed Joseph's advice. Believing that Joseph had been given wisdom by God, the king appointed him governor of Egypt, giving him more authority than anyone except himself.

After seven years of good harvests, a famine arrived. Joseph's brothers came to Egypt looking for grain so they would not starve. Joseph met with them, but they did not recognise the brother they had sold into slavery. Joseph decided to have some fun by pretending to think that they were spies, but eventually he revealed his true identity. The brothers were truly glad to see him alive. Jacob also came to Egypt and was reunited with his son. God changed Jacob's name to Israel, and the families of his sons became known as the **Twelve Tribes of Israel**.

Jacob's sons

The Twelve Tribes of Israel were named after Jacob's sons:

Reuben
Simeon
Levi
Judah
Dan
Naphtali
Gad
Asher
Issachar
Zebulun
Joseph
Benjamin

Key vocabulary

cup-bearer Someone who serves wine in a royal household
Twelve Tribes of Israel The name given to the families and descendants of Jacob's sons

Check your understanding

1 How did Potiphar's wife get Joseph into trouble?
2 How did Joseph help the baker and cup-bearer while he was in prison?
3 Explain what happened in one of the king's dreams and what the dream meant.
4 How did the king reward Joseph for interpreting his dreams?
5 What happened when Joseph's brothers visited Egypt?

Unit 1: Old Testament: Genesis
Knowledge organiser

Key vocabulary

ark The ship built by Noah to survive the flood

bless To award God's protection and favour to someone

circumcise To remove a male's foreskin

covenant An agreement or promise between God and people

cup-bearer Someone who serves wine in a royal household

descendant A future relation, for example, a child or child's child

faith Trust in God

the Fall Adam and Eve's disobedience towards God by eating the forbidden fruit, bringing sin and evil into the world

Garden of Eden The garden created by God for Adam and Eve to live in

Genesis The first book in the Bible; it literally means 'origin'

Israelites The name given to Abraham's descendants, chosen by God to be a great nation and have their own land

myth A story that is not historically true, but that contains spiritual truth

New Testament The second part of the Bible, written around CE 30–70

Old Testament The first part of the Bible, written between 800 BCE and 165 BCE

original sin The Christian belief that everybody is born with a desire to do wrong

Pentateuch The first five books of the Bible: Genesis, Exodus, Leviticus, Numbers and Deuteronomy

sacrifice An animal or other farming product dedicated to God as a way of thanking him, saying sorry or asking for protection

scriptures Religious texts

sin Disobeying God

Torah The name, meaning 'law', that Jewish people give to the first five books of the Bible, the most important Jewish scriptures

Twelve Tribes of Israel The name given to the families and descendants of Jacob's sons

Adam and Eve eating the forbidden fruit.

Key facts

- The Bible is a collection of 66 or more separate books written by about 40 different authors over a period of several centuries. These books are organised into two sections – the Old Testament and the New Testament.

- Christians believe that the Bible is inspired by God. Some interpret the Bible literally and others think that some of its stories are myths.

- The first book of the Bible is called Genesis, a word that means 'origin'. The first chapter of Genesis explains the origin of the universe.

- In Genesis, God creates the first humans, Adam and Eve, and tells them they can eat the fruit from any tree in the Garden of Eden except the tree that 'gives knowledge of good and evil'. They disobey him, and Christians believe this brought original sin into the world.

- Adam and Eve had sons called Cain and Abel. Christians believe the effects of original sin can be seen in Cain's murder of his brother Abel.

- According to Genesis, as the earth's population increased, so too did the amount of violence and evil. God decided to send a great flood to wipe out the human race, but he told a good man named Noah to build an ark to save himself and his family.

- God wanted to establish a special nation of people who would follow his laws and be an example to all others. He chose a man named Abraham to be the father of this nation. He tested Abraham's suitability by asking him to sacrifice his son, Isaac.

- Isaac had twin sons, Jacob and Esau. Jacob had 12 of his own sons, including Joseph. Joseph's brothers disliked him because he was his father's favourite and dreamed of his brothers bowing down to him.

- Joseph's brothers sold him into slavery in Egypt, where he worked for Potiphar before being imprisoned when Potiphar's wife accused him of trying to get into bed with her. He was released from prison after interpreting the king's dreams. The king made him the second most powerful man in Egypt.

The snake, who tempts Eve into disobeying God, is often believed to symbolise the devil.

Key people

Abel Adam and Eve's son, who is murdered by his brother Cain

Abraham A man who God promises to make the 'father of a great nation'

Adam The first man in the Bible

Cain Adam and Eve's son, who murders his brother Abel

Esau Isaac's son, Jacob's brother

Eve The first woman in the Bible

Isaac Abraham's son, who God tells Abraham to sacrifice as a test of his faith

Jacob Isaac's son, who has 12 sons himself who create the Twelve Tribes of Israel

Joseph A son of Jacob, who is sold into slavery in Egypt by his brothers because of the dreams he has about them

Noah A man called by God to build an ark to save him from the flood

Potiphar A man who Joseph works for in Egypt

Old Testament: Exodus to exile

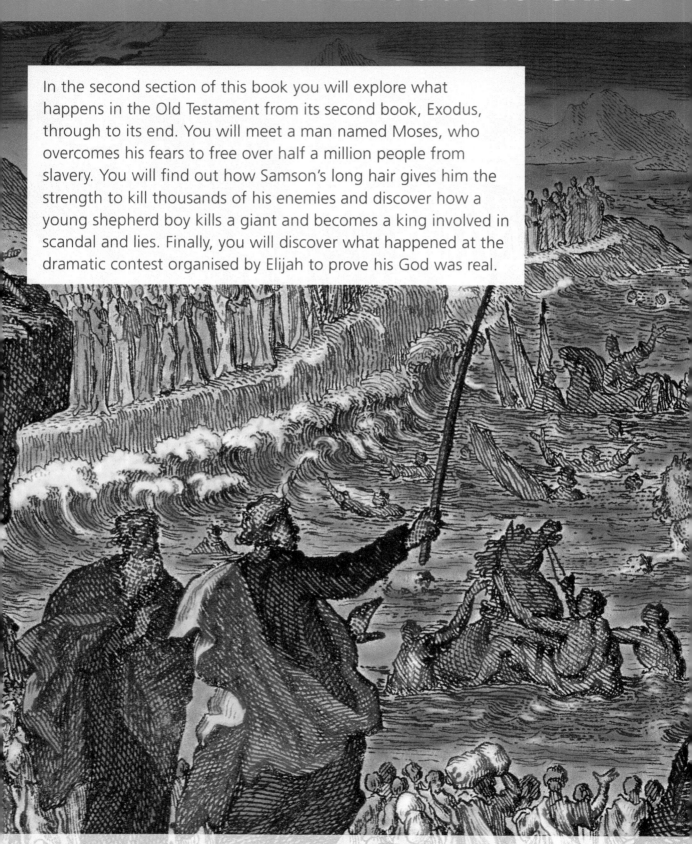

In the second section of this book you will explore what happens in the Old Testament from its second book, Exodus, through to its end. You will meet a man named Moses, who overcomes his fears to free over half a million people from slavery. You will find out how Samson's long hair gives him the strength to kill thousands of his enemies and discover how a young shepherd boy kills a giant and becomes a king involved in scandal and lies. Finally, you will discover what happened at the dramatic contest organised by Elijah to prove his God was real.

Unit 2: Old Testament: Exodus to exile
The early life of Moses

The second book of the Bible, Exodus, begins with the king of Egypt trying to drown all the Israelite babies. How did Moses survive?

Killer king

By the beginning of the second book of the Bible, Exodus, the Israelites were living in Egypt as slaves. Despite this, they were a strong people, and their population was increasing. The king of Egypt was concerned that if war broke out the Israelites might join forces with the Egyptians' enemies. He made them work long, gruelling hours in the cornfields or constructing buildings, hoping that this would stop them reproducing, but the Israelites continued to increase.

The king came up with a new plan. He ordered the midwives who delivered the Israelites' babies to kill all the boys, but the midwives refused. Next, the king commanded all his people to throw any new born Israelite boys into the river Nile so that they would drown.

The Birth of Moses

2 " [1] During this time a man from the tribe of Levi married a woman of his own tribe, [2] and she bore him a son. When she saw what a fine baby he was, she hid him for three months. [3] But when she could not hide him any longer, she took a basket made of reeds and covered it with tar to make it watertight. She put the baby in it and then placed it in the tall grass at the edge of the river. [4] The baby's sister stood some distance away to see what would happen to him. "

" [5] The king's daughter came down to the river to bathe, while her servants walked along the bank. Suddenly she noticed the basket in the tall grass and sent a slave woman to get it. [6] The princess opened it and saw a baby boy. He was crying, and she felt sorry for him. 'This is one of the Hebrew* babies,' she said. "

" [7] Then his sister asked her, 'Shall I go and call a Hebrew woman to act as a wet nurse?' "

" [8] 'Please do,' she answered. So the girl went and brought the baby's own mother. [9] The princess told the woman, 'Take this baby and nurse him for me, and I will pay you.' So she took the baby and nursed him. [10] Later, when the child was old enough, she took him to the king's daughter, who adopted him as her own son. She said to herself, 'I pulled him out of the water, and so I name him Moses.' "

Moses escapes to Midian

" [11] When Moses had grown up, he went out to visit his people, the Hebrews, and he saw how they were forced to do hard labour. He even saw an Egyptian kill a Hebrew, one of Moses' own people. [12] Moses looked all around, and when he saw that no one was watching, he killed the Egyptian and hid his body in the sand. [13] The next day he went back and saw two Hebrew men fighting. He said to the one who was in the wrong, 'Why are you beating up a fellow-Hebrew?' "

> " [14] The man answered, 'Who made you our ruler and judge? Are you going to kill me just as you killed that Egyptian?' Then Moses was afraid and said to himself, 'People have found out what I have done.' [15-16] When the king heard about what had happened, he tried to have Moses killed, but Moses fled and went to live in the land of Midian. "

Exodus 2.1–16

* Israelite

Moses being rescued from the river as a baby.

Moses sees a Hebrew slave being murdered.

Moses and the Torah

In the past, many people believed that Moses wrote the first five books of the Bible – the Pentateuch, or the Torah in Judaism. Nowadays, however, most biblical scholars think that there were probably a number of different authors. They probably wrote the stories after they had been passed down through word of mouth in the centuries after Moses' death. One reason that scholars think that there was more than one author is because there is quite a lot of repetition in these books, which suggests different people writing about the same event. There also seems to be different styles of writing and different vocabulary within the Torah. In addition, the death of Moses is mentioned in the Torah, suggesting that he was not the author.

Who was Moses?

Moses was a descendant of Abraham. He was a Hebrew, which is another word for an Israelite. He is an important figure in the four books that follow Genesis in the Bible: Exodus, Numbers, Leviticus and Deuteronomy. Each week at Jewish services in the **synagogue**, part of the Torah, made up of these four books plus Genesis, is read aloud. Many Jews think of Moses as the greatest **prophet** to have ever lived.

Key vocabulary

prophet A messenger from God

synagogue A Jewish place of worship

Check your understanding

1. Why was the king worried about the Israelites?
2. What did the king tell the midwives to do?
3. How did Moses survive as a baby?
4. Why did Moses run away to the land of Midian?
5. Give two reasons why most biblical scholars today do not think that Moses wrote the Torah/Pentateuch.

Moses and the burning bush

What terrifying mission did God give to Moses while he was working as a shepherd?

In Midian, Moses became a shepherd. One day, while in the fields taking care of some sheep and goats, he saw an unusual sight. A bush was on fire, but its branches were not burning up. Moses moved closer to get a better look, and as he did so he heard a voice from the bush saying, 'I am the God of your ancestors, the God of Abraham, Isaac and Jacob.'

66 7 Then the Lord said, 'I have seen how cruelly my people are being treated in Egypt; I have heard them cry out to be rescued from their slave-drivers. I know all about their sufferings, 8 and so I have come down to rescue them from the Egyptians and to bring them out of Egypt to a spacious land, one which is rich and fertile and in which the Canaanites, the Hittites, the Amorites, the Perizzites, the Hivites, and the Jebusites now live. 9 I have indeed heard the cry of my people, and I see how the Egyptians are oppressing them. 10 Now I am sending you to the king of Egypt so that you can lead my people out of his country.' 99

66 11 But Moses said to God, 'I am nobody. How can I go to the king and bring the Israelites out of Egypt?' 99

66 12 God answered, 'I will be with you, and when you bring the people out of Egypt, you will worship me on this mountain. That will be the proof that I have sent you.' 99

66 13 But Moses replied, 'When I go to the Israelites and say to them, "The God of your ancestors sent me to you," they will ask me, "What is his name?" So what can I tell them?' 99

66 14 God said, 'I am who I am. This is what you must say to them: "The one who is called I AM has sent me to you." 15 Tell the Israelites that I, the Lord, the God of their ancestors, the God of Abraham, Isaac, and Jacob, have sent you to them. This is my name forever; this is what all future generations are to call me. 16 Go and gather the leaders of Israel together and tell them that I, the Lord, the God of their ancestors, the God of Abraham, Isaac, and Jacob, appeared to you. Tell them that I have come to them and have seen what the Egyptians are doing to them. 17 I have decided that I will bring them out of Egypt, where they are being treated cruelly, and will take them to a rich and fertile land – the land of the Canaanites, the Hittites, the Amorites, the Perizzites, the Hivites, and the Jebusites. 99

66 18 'My people will listen to what you say to them. Then you must go with the leaders of Israel to the king of Egypt and say to him, "The Lord, the God of the Hebrews, has revealed himself to us. Now allow us to travel three days into the desert to offer sacrifices to the Lord, our God." 19 I know that the king of Egypt will not let you go unless he is forced to do so. 20 But I will use my power and will punish Egypt by doing terrifying things there. After that he will let you go.' 99

Exodus 3.7–20

Moses and the burning bush.

A talking bush and a terrifying mission

As Moses stood before the burning bush, God told him he was giving him the task of freeing the Israelites from slavery in Egypt. Moses was terrified. He was just a shepherd! He was not a good speaker. How would he get people to listen to him? He did not think he was the right man for the job.

Moses pleaded with God to send someone else, but eventually he gave in. God told him that he would lead the Israelites to a new 'rich and fertile' land. However, Moses could see another problem – there were already seven other tribes living in the land that God had promised to give to the Israelites. God reassured Moses that he would help the Israelites conquer the tribes, so Moses reluctantly accepted his mission and set off back to Egypt.

The story of Moses and the burning bush is often thought to show that God was concerned about the fact that his chosen people were living in slavery. He wanted to prove that he had not forgotten his covenant with Abraham – that his descendants would have their own special land.

Snakes and skin disease

In chapter 4 of Exodus, God gives Moses the power to perform two signs to prove to the Israelites that he has been sent by God. First, God tells Moses to throw his staff on the ground, causing it to turn into a snake. Moses runs away, but God tells him to pick the snake up by the tail. When Moses picks it up, it turns back into a staff. Second, God tells Moses to put his hand inside his cloak. When he does this, his hand shows signs of **leprosy**. God tells Moses to put it back inside his cloak and then take it out again. When Moses does so, he is cured.

Michelangelo's statue of Moses in Rome, Italy.

Key vocabulary

leprosy A skin disease

Check your understanding

1. What is unusual about the bush in this story?
2. What does God tell Moses to do and why is Moses reluctant?
3. In what ways does Moses show strong faith?
4. What two miraculous signs does God give Moses the power to perform?
5. How is God's covenant with Abraham linked to this story?

The 10 plagues and the exodus

At first, the king of Egypt was unwilling to free the Israelites from slavery. What did God do to change the king's mind?

Moses returns to Egypt

Moses followed God's instructions and returned to Egypt. He told the Israelite leaders everything that God had said to him and he showed them the two miraculous signs that God had given him. The Israelites believed that God had sent Moses and they bowed down and worshipped God.

Moses went to the king of Egypt and asked him to give the Israelites three days off so they could worship God in the desert. The king refused. He thought the Israelites were just being lazy, so he ordered the slave masters to make life even more difficult for them. So they could not make bricks, they were given no straw, which made building work impossible. When they failed to build, the slave masters beat them. The Israelites soon turned against Moses. All he had done was make their lives even harder.

When Moses complained to God, God assured him that he had not forgotten his covenant. Moses told the Israelites what God had said, but they would no longer listen to him. Moses tried once more to persuade the king to let the Israelites go, by performing the miracle of turning his staff into a snake. Still the king refused.

God sent 10 plagues to Egypt because the king refused to free the Israelites from slavery.

As God had warned, he sent **10 plagues** to Egypt. When his son died in the 10th plague, the king gave in. He told Moses to gather the Israelites and their animals and take them out of Egypt.

The exodus

The Israelites had lived in Egypt for 430 years, but now they were finally free to leave. The Bible states that Moses led 600,000 men out of Egypt as part of the **exodus** (it does not say how many women or children there were). They set off for the land that God had promised them. During the day, God showed them the way them with a pillar of cloud. At night, he directed them with a pillar of fire.

After letting the Israelites go, the king changed his mind. He sent soldiers into the desert to force the Israelites to return. As the soldiers caught up with them, the Israelites began to panic. They were on the shores of the **Red Sea** and there was no way for them to escape.

> **Activity**
>
> Make a grid of 10 boxes. In each box, draw and label an image of the 10 plagues.

> **Passover**
>
> Jews remember their ancestors being freed from slavery during the festival of **Passover**. A special meal is eaten in which each item of food represents a part of the story. For example, a mixture of nuts, wine and apples called charoset is eaten to symbolise the cement that the slaves had to make for the Egyptians. This story is important to Jews because they believe it shows that God did not forget his covenant with Abraham that his descendants would be a strong nation with their own land.

The Israelites turned on Moses, telling him it was better to be a slave than to die.

However, God had a plan. He told Moses to lift his staff and raise his hand over the sea. As Moses did so, the waves parted, so the Israelites could cross safely. When the Egyptians followed the Israelites into the sea, Moses lifted his staff again, and the water flowed back, covering the Egyptian army. When the Israelites saw this, they put their trust in God and in their leader, Moses.

Moses parting the Red Sea.

The 10 plagues

1. A river of blood. The Nile turned to blood. The fish died, the river stank and the Egyptians could not drink its water.

2. A plague of frogs. They got into everyone's homes and even the king's palace.

3. All the dust in Egypt turned into fleas.

4. Swarms of flies.

5. A plague on livestock, which killed all the horses, donkeys, camels, cattle, sheep and goats.

6. A plague of boils on all the men and animals in the land.

7. A plague of hail that killed all people and animals caught outside in the storm.

8. A plague of locusts, which covered the ground, filled houses and ate the trees.

9. A plague of darkness across the whole of Egypt for three days.

10. A plague on the firstborn. God told Moses that he was going to kill the firstborn son of every Egyptian, including the king's son. He told Moses to tell the Israelites to put the blood of a lamb on the top and both sides of their doors, so that the destroyer would pass over those houses and cause no harm. At midnight, all the firstborn sons were killed.

Key vocabulary

exodus The Israelites' journey out of Egypt

Passover A Jewish festival remembering the Israelites' freedom from slavery in Egypt

Red Sea A narrow sea that lies between Africa and Asia; in Exodus, the sea is parted so the Israelites can cross it safely and escape from the Egyptians

The 10 plagues The 10 disasters that God inflicted on the people of Egypt to convince the king to free the Israelites

Check your understanding

1 Why did the king not want to let the Israelites go?

2 Which three plagues do you think would have been the worst? Why do you think this?

3 Explain why the king eventually freed the Israelites.

4 What happened at the Red Sea?

5 Discuss how the Israelites responded to Moses trying to free them.

Unit 2: Old Testament: Exodus to exile

The Ten Commandments

Life in a desert community came with many challenges. God gave the Israelites commandments to help them live peacefully with one another and to stay faithful to him, but how easy would it be to follow these?

Moses receives the commandments

Three months after leaving Egypt, the Israelites were camping in the desert near a mountain called Mount Sinai. The Israelites were God's chosen people and they had a special relationship with him. He had made a covenant with their ancestor Abraham that he would protect them and give them their own land in which to live. God wanted to make it clear to the Israelites how they should live and honour him, so he called Moses to meet him on Mount Sinai. He gave him 10 rules, known as the **Ten Commandments**, or 'the law'. They were engraved on two stone tablets.

Mount Sinai is now considered a holy place and is a site of pilgrimage.

While Moses was away, the Israelites began worshipping a golden statue of a calf that they had made out of their jewellery. When Moses saw this, he was furious, and smashed the two stone tablets into pieces. He burned the golden calf to powder and made the Israelites drink the powder in their water. Moses then returned to God on Mount Sinai and once again received the Ten Commandments on two stone tablets.

The Ten Commandments

1. You shall have no other gods before me.

2. You shall not bow down to or worship any image.

3. You shall not misuse the name of the Lord your God.

4. Remember the **Sabbath** day and keep it holy.

5. Honour your father and mother.

6. You shall not murder.

7. You shall not commit **adultery**.

8. You shall not steal.

9. You shall not give false testimony against your neighbour.

10. You shall not **covet** your neighbour's house, wife, servants, ox or donkey or anything that belongs to your neighbour.

The meaning of the commandments

At this time there were many tribes in the area who prayed to different gods. They would make statues of their gods and worship them.

The first two commandments warned the Israelites that they must be committed to the one God who had rescued them from Egypt and that they must not make statues of him or any other gods. This is why Moses was so angry when the Israelites made the golden calf.

The third commandment warned against making false promises using God's name. Today, this commandment is believed to include swearing or using God's name disrespectfully.

The Israelites were living in the desert and, as former slaves, their possessions were not luxuries but were the things they needed to survive. If they lost these essential items they might die, so ensuring that everyone kept the eighth commandment, 'You shall not steal', was very important.

The ninth commandment states that the Israelites must not give false testimony. This means they must not lie about what someone has done. In ancient desert communities, if someone witnessed a crime, they were usually responsible for killing the guilty person. This was not considered murder by the law. The ninth commandment therefore ensured that an innocent person would not be executed.

The word 'covet' in the 10th commandment means to want something that is not yours. It is similar to jealousy. This commandment made sure that the Israelites lived in peace and harmony with their neighbours.

Spies and giants

When the Israelites arrived at the edge of Canaan, the land that God had promised them, Moses sent 12 spies ahead to see what the area was like. They returned with bad news. They reported that the people living in Canaan were huge and the Israelites stood no chance of defeating them and settling in this country. Rumours started to spread among the Israelites of giants living in Canaan. They were angry with Moses for leading them there, and some Israelites even threatened to stone him to death. God decided that these Israelites would not enter the **promised land**, because of their lack of faith.

For another 40 years, the Israelites wandered the desert, trying to avoid being attacked by other tribes. Eventually, a whole generation died, including Moses himself. A man named Joshua became leader of the Israelites, and it was he who eventually led them into the land that God had promised them.

Activity

In pairs, discuss whether you think the Ten Commandments are a good guide of how people should live today.

Key vocabulary

adultery Cheating on the person to whom you are married

covet To crave something that belongs to someone else

promised land The land of Canaan, which God promised to give to the Israelites

Sabbath The seventh day of the week, reserved for religious activities, when people do not work

Ten Commandments The 10 rules given by God to Moses for the Israelites to follow

Check your understanding

1. What did the Israelites do while Moses was on Mount Sinai?
2. What did Moses do after returning to the Israelites from Mount Sinai?
3. Which other commandments might someone break if he or she were coveting?
4. What do you think the Israelite community would have been like if everybody followed the Ten Commandments?
5. 'Moses was a great leader of the Israelites.' Discuss this statement.

Unit 2: Old Testament: Exodus to exile
The Judges

After the Israelites settled in the promised land, they began to forget God's teachings. To help and guide them, God sent them strong leaders known as the Judges. Why did one of these men, Samson, cause such a commotion?

Life in Canaan

Under Joshua's leadership, the Israelites conquered large parts of Canaan. However, some other tribes remained in the area, and these tribes worshipped their own gods. After Joshua and his generation died, the Israelites began to forget all that God had done for them. They broke the Ten Commandments and worshipped the gods of the Canaanite tribes. When life became difficult, however, they would plead with God to send them leaders who could rescue them. These were the Judges, and their stories are told in the seventh book of the Old Testament.

> 66 Then the people of Israel sinned against the Lord and began to serve the **Baals**. 12 They stopped worshipping the Lord, the God of their ancestors, the God who had brought them out of Egypt, and they began to worship other gods, the gods of the peoples around them. They bowed down to them and made the Lord angry. 13 They stopped worshipping the Lord and served the Baals and the Astartes. 14 And so the Lord became furious with Israel and let raiders attack and rob them. He let the enemies all around overpower them, and the Israelites could no longer protect themselves. 15 Every time they would go into battle, the Lord was against them, just as he had said he would be. They were in great distress. 99

> 66 16 Then the Lord gave the Israelites leaders who saved them from the raiders. 17 But the Israelites paid no attention to their leaders. Israel was unfaithful to the Lord and worshipped other gods. Their fathers had obeyed the Lord's commands, but this new generation soon stopped doing so. 18 Whenever the Lord gave Israel a leader, the Lord would help that leader and would save the people from their enemies as long as that leader lived. The Lord would have mercy on them because they groaned under their suffering and oppression. 19 But when the leader died, the people would return to the old ways and behave worse than the previous generation. They would serve and worship other gods, and refused to give up their own evil ways. 20 Then the Lord would become furious with Israel and say, 'This nation has broken the covenant that I commanded their ancestors to keep. Because they have not obeyed me, 21 I will no longer drive out any of the nations that were still in the land when Joshua died. 22 I will use them to find out whether or not these Israelites will follow my ways, as their ancestors did.' 99
>
> Judges 2.11–22

Super-strong Samson

One of the Judges was an incredibly strong man named Samson. The secret to his strength was that he never cut his hair. Samson married a **Philistine** woman rather than an Israelite. One day Samson went to his wife's room to visit her. However, her father had been sure that Samson hated her, and so had let another man be with her. The father offered Samson his younger daughter, but would not let Samson see his wife. Samson was furious and decided he was going to take revenge on the Philistines. He went out and caught 300 foxes and tied their tails together with branches. He then set fire to the branches and released the foxes in the Philistines' fields of ripe grain, burning all their crops.

Samson was so fearless that he once tore a lion apart with his bare hands.

When the Philistines found out that Samson was responsible for the damage, they burned his wife and his wife's father. In revenge, Samson killed many Philistines before going into hiding in a cave. Eventually, he was discovered there, tied up and taken to the Philistines. Samson broke free, however, and, spotting a donkey's jawbone on the floor, he picked it up and used it to kill 1000 men. Afterwards he said to himself: 'With this donkey's jawbone, I have made donkeys out of all these people.'

After his first marriage, Samson fell in love with another Philistine woman. She tricked Samson into telling her the secret of his strength and then, while he slept, she shaved his head. When Samson woke, he found the room full of Philistines. He stood up to attack them, but discovered that all his strength had gone. The Philistines gouged out his eyes and then held him as a prisoner.

Over time, Samson's hair began to grow back. One day, during a feast in their temple, the Philistines carried Samson out in chains to be mocked in public. Although he was blind, Samson's strength had returned, as his hair had grown. Samson grabbed two main pillars in the temple and brought the building crashing down. All 3000 people inside were killed, including Samson himself.

Samson tearing down the Philistine temple.

Key vocabulary

Baal A god worshipped by the Canaanite tribes
Philistine A member of a tribe that fought against the Israelites

Check your understanding

1. Who led the Israelites into the promised land?
2. What happened after the Israelites settled in Canaan?
3. How did God respond to the Israelites' disobedience in Judges 2.16–22?
4. What mistake did Samson make twice?
5. What happened in the temple?

Unit 2: Old Testament: Exodus to exile
David and Goliath

The Israelites were at war with the Philistines. They were especially afraid of a Philistine named Goliath. What happened when a young Israelite boy named David took on this giant of a man?

Goliath's challenge

Goliath was over 2.8 metres (9 feet) tall, wore heavy armour and he carried an enormous spear. Every morning for 40 days, he challenged the Israelites to send their best fighter against him. If an Israelite won, Goliath said that he and the Philistines would become the Israelites' slaves. If he won, then the Israelites would have to become the Philistines' slaves.

One day, a young Israelite shepherd boy called David heard Goliath bellowing his morning challenge. David watched as the fearful Israelites ran away and then he asked them: 'Why are you so frightened of Goliath, when God is on your side?' The Israelites told David to go back to his sheep, but news of what he had said reached Saul, the king of Israel. He sent for David.

David told Saul that when lions and bears had tried to steal his father's lambs and attack him, he grabbed them by the throat and beat them to death. He told Saul that he would do the same to Goliath. Saul was concerned because David was just a boy, whereas Goliath had been a soldier all his life, but he agreed to give David his armour, helmet and sword. David tried these on, but he was unused to heavy armour and could not walk in it. He decided to battle Goliath with just his shepherd's stick, five stones and a sling.

> **Fact**
>
> After many years of having Judges as leaders, the Israelites decided they wanted a king instead, like other nations. God gave them a king called Saul, which in Hebrew means 'the one asked for' or 'requested'.

David defeats Goliath

❝ 41The Philistine started walking toward David, with his shield-bearer walking in front of him. He kept coming closer, 42 and when he got a good look at David, he was filled with scorn for him because he was just a nice, good-looking boy. 43 He said to David, 'What's that stick for? Do you think I'm a dog?' And he called down curses from his god on David. 44 'Come on,' he challenged David, 'and I will give your body to the birds and animals to eat.' ❞

❝ 45 David answered, 'You are coming against me with sword, spear, and javelin, but I come against you in the name of the Lord Almighty, the God of the Israelite armies, which you have defied. 46 This very day the Lord will put you in my power; I will defeat you and cut off your head. And I will give the bodies of the Philistine soldiers to the birds and animals to eat. Then the whole world will know that Israel has a God, 47 and everyone here will see that the Lord does not need swords or spears to save his people. He is victorious in battle, and he will put all of you in our power.' ❞

> [48] Goliath started walking toward David again, and David ran quickly toward the Philistine battle line to fight him. [49] He reached into his bag and took out a stone, which he slung at Goliath. It hit him on the forehead and broke his skull, and Goliath fell face downwards on the ground. [50] And so, without a sword, David defeated and killed Goliath with a sling and a stone! [51] He ran to him, stood over him, took Goliath's sword out of its sheath, and cut off his head and killed him. When the Philistines saw that their hero was dead, they ran away.

1 Samuel 17.41–51

David fights Goliath.

David the king

David married Saul's daughter and became close friends with the king's son, Jonathan. However, Saul became jealous of David's popularity. One night, Saul threw a spear at David in an attempt to kill him. David escaped and hid in caves.

Later, David found himself living among the Philistines. Worried that they would take revenge for the death of Goliath, he pretended to be mad so that they would leave him alone. Eventually, Saul and Jonathan were killed in battle by the Philistines, and this allowed David to return home. There he was chosen as the second king of Israel.

During his time as king, David defeated the Philistines and other tribes. He turned Jerusalem into a wonderful capital city. Things seemed to be going well for the Israelites. God had not forgotten his covenant with Abraham and now he made a new covenant with David, promising that his 'throne would last forever'. This meant that David's descendants would always be the kings of God's people.

The statue of David

This famous sculpture called *David* was created by Italian artist Michelangelo in 1501–04. This was the first time an artist had depicted David before, rather than after, the battle with Goliath. David looks tense and is concentrating hard, but he is also standing in a confident, relaxed and alert position. The sling he is carrying over his shoulder is almost invisible. This was to show that he did not win because of his strength or power, but because of his belief.

Michelangelo's statue of David.

Activity

Imagine you were a spectator as David fought Goliath. Write a battlefield report of David's victory.

Check your understanding

1 Why were the Israelites afraid of Goliath?

2 Why was David confident that he would defeat Goliath?

3 Why did David run away after his victory?

4 What covenant did God made with David?

5 Do you think that Michelangelo shows David's character in his statue?

David and Bathsheba

How did David try to cover up his wrong doing after committing adultery with Bathsheba?

David misses a battle

The Old Testament writings portray King David as someone who trusted in God and was rewarded for his faith. As king, it was David's job to lead the Israelites in battle and protect them from their enemies. One day, however, David decided not to go into battle. He sent his army chief, Joab, to lead the battle instead.

> 11   1 The following spring, at the time of the year when kings usually go to war, David sent out Joab with his officers and the Israelite army; they defeated the Ammonites and besieged the city of Rabbah. But David himself stayed in Jerusalem.
>
> 2 One day, late in the afternoon, David got up from his nap and went to the palace roof. As he walked around up there, he saw a woman taking a bath in her house. She was very beautiful. 3 So he sent a messenger to find out who she was, and learnt that she was Bathsheba, the daughter of Eliam and the wife of Uriah the Hittite. 4 David sent messengers to get her; they brought her to him and he made love to her. (She had just finished her monthly ritual of purification.) Then she went back home. 5 Afterwards she discovered that she was pregnant and sent a message to David to tell him.
>
> 6 David then sent a message to Joab: 'Send me Uriah the Hittite.' So Joab sent him to David. 7 When Uriah arrived, David asked him if Joab and the troops were well, and how the fighting was going. 8 Then he said to Uriah, 'Go on home and rest a while.' Uriah left, and David had a present sent to his home. 9 But Uriah did not go home; instead he slept at the palace gate with the king's guards.
>
> 10 When David heard that Uriah had not gone home, he asked him, 'You have just returned after a long absence; why didn't you go home?'
>
> 11 Uriah answered, 'The men of Israel and Judah are away in battle, and the **Covenant Box** is with them; my commander Joab and his officers are camping out in the open. How could I go home, eat and drink, and sleep with my wife? By all that's sacred, I swear that I could never do such a thing!'
>
> 12 So David said, 'Then stay here the rest of the day, and tomorrow I'll send you back.' So Uriah stayed in Jerusalem that day and the next. 13 David invited him to supper and made him drunk. But again that night Uriah did not go home; instead he slept on his blanket in the palace guardroom.
>
> 14 The next morning David wrote a letter to Joab and sent it by Uriah. 15 He wrote: 'Put Uriah in the front line, where the fighting is heaviest, then retreat and let him be killed.' 16 So while Joab was besieging the city, he sent Uriah to a place where he knew the enemy was strong. 17 The enemy troops came out of the city and fought Joab's forces; some of David's officers were killed, and so was Uriah.
>
> 2 Samuel 11.1–17

Activity

Draw a table with two columns. On one side, list as many reasons as you can why someone might say that Moses was a better leader of the Israelites than David. On the other side, give reasons why David could be seen as the better leader. You could write up your ideas as an essay.

This tapestry shows Bathsheba arriving at King David's court.

A royal scandal

After Uriah's death, David married Bathsheba and they had a son, but God was displeased with what David had done. A prophet called Nathan visited David and asked him why he had behaved in this way when he was already so fortunate. As David spoke to Nathan, he felt regret at how he had sinned and caused harm to his people. Nathan told David that God forgave him, but that as a consequence of his actions David's son would die, his descendants would be violent and he would be humiliated by other men sleeping with his wives.

Years later, one of David's sons, Absalom, gathered an army to fight his father. During the battle, Absalom's entire army was killed. While trying to escape, Absalom's head got caught in the branches of a tree and he died there.

Solomon and his many wives

Despite David's sin, God kept his promise to David that someone from his family line would always be king of Israel. After David's death, his son Solomon became king. Things started well for Solomon. He built a magnificent temple in Jerusalem for the Israelites to worship God, and he was known for his wisdom. However, Solomon had 700 wives who worshipped many different gods. By the end of his life, Solomon had turned away from his own God, and had started worshipping the gods of his wives.

When two women both claimed that a baby was theirs, Solomon showed his wisdom by ordering the baby to be chopped in half and shared. The real mother would not let this happen, and in this way Solomon knew the baby was hers.

Psalms

The book of Psalms is one of the longest books in the Bible. It contains 150 songs that the Israelites sang to worship God. David was a poet and musician who is credited with writing some of the Psalms. Psalm 51 is David's prayer for forgiveness after sinning with Bathsheba. Solomon also wrote a book of wise sayings called Proverbs. This book comes straight after Psalms in the Old Testament.

Key vocabulary

Covenant Box A special box containing the stone tablets on which the Ten Commandments were inscribed

Check your understanding

1 Which of the Ten Commandments did David break?
2 David made three plans to try and cover up his adultery. What were they?
3 What happened when Nathan visited David?
4 What sort of king was Solomon?
5 David is often seen as one of the Bible's heroes. Do you think this is deserved?

Elijah and exile

What happened when Elijah challenged the prophets of Baal to a contest to see whose God was real?

Elijah the prophet

After Solomon's death, Israel split into two kingdoms. The northern tribes kept the name Israel while the southern kingdom became known as Judah. Each kingdom had its own king. Many of the kings abandoned God and worshipped the gods of the tribes around them, so God decided to send prophets to remind them of him. One of these prophets was Elijah.

At this time, an evil man named Ahab was king of Israel. He was married to Jezebel, who was even more cruel than her husband. She drove all the prophets into hiding and replaced them with prophets of Baal, the Canaanite god whom the Israelites had started to worship. Elijah challenged the prophets of Baal to a contest.

> ❝ 20 So Ahab summoned all the Israelites and the prophets of Baal to meet at Mount Carmel. 21 Elijah went up to the people and said, 'How much longer will it take you to make up your minds? If the Lord is God, worship him; but if Baal is God, worship him!' But the people didn't say a word. 22 Then Elijah said, 'I am the only prophet of the Lord still left, but there are 450 prophets of Baal. 23 Bring two bulls; let the prophets of Baal take one, kill it, cut it in pieces, and put it on the wood – but don't light the fire. I will do the same with the other bull. 24 Then let the prophets of Baal pray to their god, and I will pray to the Lord, and the one who answers by sending fire – he is God.' ❞

The people shouted their approval

> ❝ 25 Then Elijah said to the prophets of Baal, 'Since there are so many of you, you take a bull and prepare it first. Pray to your god, but don't set fire to the wood.' ❞

> ❝ 26 They took the bull that was brought to them, prepared it, and prayed to Baal until noon. They shouted, 'Answer us, Baal!' and kept dancing around the altar they had built. But no answer came. ❞

> ❝ 27 At noon Elijah started making fun of them: 'Pray louder! He is a god! Maybe he is day-dreaming or relieving himself, or perhaps he's gone on a journey! Or maybe he's sleeping, and you've got to wake him up!' 28 So the prophets prayed louder and cut themselves with knives and daggers, according to their ritual, until blood flowed. 29 They kept on ranting and raving until the middle of the afternoon; but no answer came, not a sound was heard. ❞

Elijah defeating the prophets of Baal.

💬 30 Then Elijah said to the people, 'Come closer to me,' and they all gathered around him. He set about repairing the altar of the Lord which had been torn down. 31 He took twelve stones, one for each of the twelve tribes named for the sons of Jacob, the man to whom the Lord had given the name Israel. 32 With these stones he rebuilt the altar for the worship of the Lord. He dug a trench around it, large enough to hold almost fourteen litres of water. 33 Then he placed the wood on the altar, cut the bull in pieces, and laid it on the wood. He said, 'Fill four jars with water and pour it on the offering and the wood.' They did so, 34 and he said, 'Do it again' – and they did. 'Do it once more,' he said – and they did. 35 The water ran down around the altar and filled the trench. 💬

💬 36 At the hour of the afternoon sacrifice the prophet Elijah approached the altar and prayed, 'O Lord, the God of Abraham, Isaac, and Jacob, prove now that you are the God of Israel and that I am your servant and have done all this at your command. 37 Answer me, Lord, answer me, so that this people will know that you, the Lord, are God and that you are bringing them back to yourself.' 💬

💬 38 The Lord sent fire down, and it burned up the sacrifice, the wood, and the stones, scorched the earth and dried up the water in the trench. 39 When the people saw this, they threw themselves on the ground and exclaimed, 'The Lord is God; the Lord alone is God!' 💬

💬 40 Elijah ordered, 'Seize the prophets of Baal; don't let any of them get away!' The people seized them all, and Elijah led them down to the River Kishon and killed them. 💬

1 Kings 18.20–40

The Israelites were treated badly under the rule of the Babylonian king Nebuchadnezzar.

Exile again

After Elijah's death, God continued to send prophets to Israel. However, the Israelites continued to forget their God and act wickedly. During this time, both kingdoms were invaded by foreign powers. Solomon's temple in Jerusalem was destroyed and the Israelites were forced out of their homes and their land. Once again, they found themselves living in **exile**, in a place called Babylon. The Babylonian king was the wicked Nebuchadnezzar, who forced the Israelites to worship a large gold statue of him. The Babylonians taunted the Israelites about the fact that their God had abandoned them.

Eventually, the Babylonians were defeated by the Persians. The Persians allowed the Israelites to return to their land, but life was tough for them. They longed for the days when they were a strong nation under King David and hoped that God would send them a **Messiah** to defeat the rulers of their land and make them strong again. During this time, the Israelites became known as **Jews**. This name originated from the southern kingdom of Judah, where the descendants of Jacob's son Judah lived.

Key vocabulary

exile Being forced to live outside the country of your birth

Jew The name given to the Israelites' descendants today

Messiah A saviour, or rescuer, sent by God

Check your understanding

1 Why did God send prophets to the Israelites?

2 Describe what happened on Mount Carmel.

3 Why did the Israelites end up in exile and what was it like for them?

4 What were the Israelites hoping for at the end of the Old Testament?

5 How does God show his power in the Old Testament? Refer to Elijah and other parts of the Old Testament in your answer.

Unit 2: Old Testament: Exodus to exile
Knowledge organiser

Key vocabulary

10 plagues The 10 disasters that God inflicted on the people of Egypt to convince the king to free the Israelites

adultery Cheating on the person to whom you are married

Baal A god worshipped by the Canaanite tribes

Covenant Box A special box containing the stone tablets on which the Ten Commandments were inscribed

covet To crave something that belongs to someone else

exile Being forced to live outside the country of your birth

exodus The Israelites' journey out of Egypt

Jew The name given to the Israelites' descendants today

leprosy A skin disease

Messiah A saviour, or rescuer, sent by God

Passover A Jewish festival remembering the Israelites' freedom from slavery in Egypt

Philistine A member of a tribe that fought against the Israelites

promised land The land of Canaan, which God promised to give to the Israelites

prophet A messenger from God

Red Sea A narrow sea that lies between Africa and Asia; in Exodus, the sea is parted so the Israelites can cross it safely and escape from the Egyptians

Sabbath The seventh day of the week, reserved for religious activities, when people do not work

synagogue A Jewish place of worship

Ten Commandments The 10 rules given by God to Moses for the Israelites to follow

Key facts

- The second book of the Bible, Exodus, begins with the king of Egypt trying to drown all the Israelite babies, but Moses was saved by the king's daughter.

- Moses left Egypt to work as a shepherd in Midian because the king wanted to kill him for murdering an Egyptian.

- While looking after some sheep and goats, God spoke to Moses from a burning bush, telling him to return to Egypt and free the Israelites from slavery.

- At first, the king of Egypt was unwilling to free the Israelites from slavery, but he changed his mind after God sent 10 plagues to Egypt.

- Moses led the Israelites out of Egypt through the Red Sea and into the desert. God gave the Ten Commandments to Moses on Mount Sinai.

- Joshua led the Israelites into the land that God had promised, but the Israelites started to worship the gods of other tribes. God sent them strong leaders known as the Judges. Samson was one of the Judges, whose strength came from his long hair, which was shaved off while he slept.

- David defeated the giant Philistine Goliath with a stone and became Israel's second king after the death of Saul. While David was king he committed adultery with Bathsheba and then arranged the killing of her husband, Uriah.

- God sent the Israelites prophets like Elijah, who took part in a contest with the prophets of Baal on Mount Carmel to prove his God was real.

- The Israelites lived in exile in Babylon, where they were forced to worship King Nebuchadnezzar.

- The Israelites became known as Jews. At the end of the Old Testament, the Jews were hoping that God would send them a Messiah.

Moses showing the Ten Commandments.

Key people

Ahab The king during the time of Elijah

Bathsheba A woman with whom King David committed adultery

David A shepherd who defeated Goliath and later became the second king of Israel

Elijah A prophet who challenges the prophets of Baal to a contest

Goliath A giant Philistine man who is killed by David

Jezebel King Ahab's wicked wife, who threatened the prophets, including Elijah

Joshua The man who took over from Moses to lead the Israelites into the promised land

Moses The man God called to lead the Israelites out of Egypt and to whom God revealed the Ten Commandments

Nathan the Prophet A messenger sent to speak to David after he sins

Nebuchadnezzar The king of Babylon who makes the Israelites worship a gold statue of him

Samson One of the Judges, who was extremely strong

Saul The first king of Israel, who tried to kill David

Solomon The third king of Israel, David's son, who built the Temple in Jerusalem

Uriah the Hittite An army officer married to Bathsheba

David and Goliath.

New Testament: The life and teachings of Jesus

In the third section of this book you will examine how the New Testament records the miraculous birth of a Jew called Jesus who lived nearly 2000 years ago. You will explore his dramatic baptism and examine his encounters with the devil while living in the wilderness. You will discover the many miracles he is claimed to have performed and consider the things he taught about how people should live.

3

Unit 3: New Testament: The life and teachings of Jesus
What is the New Testament?

Who wrote the New Testament and what happens in it?

The Gospels

The Old Testament ends with the Israelites waiting for a Messiah to make them a great, strong nation, as they had been in the time of David. Four hundred years pass between events at the end of the Old Testament and the beginning of the New Testament. During this time, the Israelites became known as Jews, and their land was conquered by the Romans, who made it part of their empire. The New Testament begins with Jews living under Roman rule.

The first four books in the New Testament are named after the people who may have written them: Matthew, Mark, Luke and John. Together, they are known as the **Gospels**. Each of these books is about a man called Jesus, who lived about 2000 years ago.

Matthew's Gospel tries to show how Jesus fits the Old Testament prophets' descriptions of what the Messiah would be like. For example, he writes that Jesus was a descendant of King David and was born in Bethlehem. Both of these fit the prophets' words. Jews who believed that Jesus was the Messiah became known as Christians. Jews who did not believe that Jesus was the Messiah remained followers of Judaism.

The word 'gospel' means 'good news'.

Who was Jesus?

Jesus was born into an ordinary Jewish family. He was given an ordinary Jewish name, and when he grew up he worked in an ordinary job, as a carpenter. At this time, there were many Jewish teachers who would travel around teaching about God, and Jesus became one of them. He chose 12 **disciples**, who travelled with him around the region of Galilee.

Christians believe that Jesus was human, but they also believe he was God living on earth. The name given to God coming to earth as a human is the **incarnation**. Every year at Christmas, Christians celebrate Jesus coming into the world as a baby.

When Jesus was about 33, he was killed by the Romans. Christians believe that Jesus's death was part of God's plan. Jesus sacrificed his life to save humans from sin and death and restore the relationship between humans and God. Three days after Jesus's death, he was **resurrected** and ascended to heaven. Christians celebrate Jesus's death and resurrection at Easter.

Jesus was born in Bethlehem and died in Jerusalem. He grew up in Nazareth, and between the ages of about 30 to 33 he travelled around the region of Galilee, preaching and performing miracles.

Are the Gospels true?

Most historians agree that a man called Jesus lived 2000 years ago and that he was executed by crucifixion. However, people disagree about whether other events described in the New Testament really happened.

When considering events from hundreds or even thousands of years ago, it can be difficult to separate fact and legend. Sometimes writers want to influence the way people are remembered, so they may change or exaggerate events. For example, the Gospel writers claim that Jesus performed many miracles. Some non-religious people might say that miracles do not happen and so these parts of the Gospels cannot be true. Some Christians might respond by saying that these parts of the Gospels are myths expressing spiritual, rather than historical, truth.

The Q Source

Many biblical scholars think that both Matthew and Luke might have based some of their Gospels on an undiscovered collection of Jesus's sayings known as the Q Source. This would explain the many similarities between them. Matthew and Luke may also have based their writings on the Gospel of Mark, which most scholars think was the first Gospel to be written. This would explain the similarities between Mark's Gospel and those of Matthew and Luke.

The New Testament letters

The fifth book of the New Testament is the Acts of the Apostles. This explains how Christianity began after Jesus died. The rest of the New Testament is made up of letters written to different groups of Christians, advising them what they should believe and offering guidance on how they should live their lives. Biblical scholars think that most of the books in the New Testament were written within 70 years of Jesus's death, and some within 20 years.

Fact

Although our calendar suggests that Jesus was born in CE 1, most historians think he was born closer to 4 BCE.

Key vocabulary

disciples Jesus's 12 main followers

Gospels The first four books of the New Testament; the word 'gospel' means 'good news'

incarnation God coming to earth as a human

resurrection Coming back to life after dying

Check your understanding

1. Who were the Jews waiting for at the end of the Old Testament?
2. What are the Gospels?
3. How does the Gospel of Matthew try to show that Jesus is the Messiah?
4. What do Christians believe about Jesus?
5. Why might people debate whether the Gospels are historically accurate?

Unit 3: New Testament: The life and teachings of Jesus
The birth of Jesus

The birth of Jesus is remembered by Christians at Christmas, but how do Matthew and Luke record the events surrounding his birth?

> 66 18 This was how the birth of Jesus Christ took place. His mother Mary was engaged to Joseph, but before they were married, she found out that she was going to have a baby by the Holy Spirit. 19 Joseph was a man who always did what was right, but he did not want to disgrace Mary publicly; so he made plans to break the engagement privately. 20 While he was thinking about this, an angel of the Lord appeared to him in a dream and said, 'Joseph, descendant of David, do not be afraid to take Mary to be your wife. For it is by the Holy Spirit that she has conceived. 21 She will have a son, and you will name him Jesus – because he will save his people from their sins.' 99
>
> 66 22 Now all this happened in order to make come true what the Lord had said through the prophet 23 'A virgin will become pregnant and have a son, and he will be called Immanuel' (which means, 'God is with us.') 24 So when Joseph woke up, he married Mary, as the angel of the Lord had told him to. 25 But he had no sexual relations with her before she gave birth to her son. And Joseph named him Jesus. 99
>
> Matthew 1.18–25

According to Matthew, some wise men from the east had seen a star and so visited King Herod in Jerusalem to find out where the child who would become 'King of the Jews' had been born. Herod was concerned that there was a new king and told the wise men to let him know once they found him. The wise men followed the star to the town of **Bethlehem** and saw Jesus. They gave him gifts of gold, frankincense and myrrh. God spoke to the wise men in a dream, telling them not to go back to Herod. When Herod realised that the wise men had done this, he was furious, and ordered his troops to murder all the boys in Bethlehem under the age of two.

God spoke to Joseph in a dream, telling him that he and Mary must escape to Egypt because Herod was trying to kill Jesus. They remained in Egypt until Herod died, and then they returned to Nazareth.

Three wise men from the east visiting Herod to ask him where the new King can be found.

Similarities and differences

Mark's and John's Gospels do not mention the birth of Jesus, but there are similarities and differences between the Gospels of Matthew and Luke. In both, Mary becomes pregnant through the Holy Spirit, and Jesus is born in Bethlehem. However, Luke does not mention a star, the wise men visiting Jesus or Herod ordering all baby boys to be killed. According to Luke, Mary and Joseph were visiting Bethlehem and there were no rooms available anywhere, and so Jesus was born in a stable and laid in a manger (a feeding trough). However, Matthew says that the wise men visited him in a house. Luke also mentions shepherds who have been spoken to by angels visiting Jesus, but these events are not mentioned by Matthew.

66 [1] At that time Emperor Augustus ordered a census to be taken throughout the Roman Empire. [2] When this first census took place, Quirinius was the governor of Syria. [3] Everyone, then, went to register himself, each to his own town. 99

66 [4] Joseph went from the town of Nazareth in Galilee to the town of Bethlehem in Judea, the birthplace of King David. Joseph went there because he was a descendant of David. [5] He went to register with Mary, who was promised in marriage to him. She was pregnant, [6] and while they were in Bethlehem, the time came for her to have her baby. [7] She gave birth to her first son, wrapped him in cloths and laid him in a manger – there was no room for them to stay in the inn. 99

66 [8] There were some shepherds in that part of the country who were spending the night in the fields, taking care of their flocks. [9] An angel of the Lord appeared to them, and the glory of the Lord shone over them. They were terribly afraid, [10] but the angel said to them, 'Don't be afraid! I am here with good news for you, which will bring great joy to all the people. [11] This very day in David's town your Saviour was born – Christ the Lord! [12] And this is what will prove it to you: you will find a baby wrapped in cloths and lying in a manger.' 99

Luke 2.1–12

Fact

Despite frequently featuring in nativity plays, neither Matthew nor Luke mention Mary and Joseph travelling to Bethlehem on a donkey. Also, neither Gospel writer gives the number of wise men or shepherds, although people often think there were three of each.

According to Luke, Mary laid Jesus in a manger after he was born.

Activity

Read the first two chapters of Matthew and Luke and make a table showing the similarities and differences between them.

Key vocabulary

Bethlehem The city where Jesus was born

Check your understanding

1 How did Joseph react to Mary's pregnancy at first? What made him change his mind?
2 Why was Jesus born in Bethlehem? Why was this a problem for Mary and Joseph?
3 How did the wise men anger Herod and how did Herod respond?
4 What happens to the shepherds in Luke 2?
5 To what extent do the Gospel writers agree about the events surrounding Jesus's birth?

Unit 3: New Testament: The life and teachings of Jesus
The baptism and temptations of Jesus

At the age of about 30, Jesus was baptised and went into the wilderness, where the devil tried to tempt him. How did Jesus resist temptation?

The baptism of Jesus

In Jesus's time, there was a man known as John the Baptist because he **baptised** people in the river Jordan.

Apart from Jesus's birth, the Gospels say very little about his life before he was about 30 years old. At this age, Jesus came to the river Jordan and asked John to baptise him. At first, John refused – he thought that Jesus should be baptising *him*, not the other way around – but eventually he agreed.

A remarkable thing happened as Jesus emerged from the water after his baptism. A voice from heaven boomed, 'You are my son, whom I love; with you I am well pleased.' The Holy Spirit also descended on Jesus like a dove. After this, Jesus went into the wilderness to **fast** and pray for 40 days on his own. Christians often believe that this was to prepare him for his **ministry**. While Jesus was fasting, the devil tried to tempt him in three different ways.

> ### Fact
>
> John's taste in food and fashion were quite different from nowadays. The Gospel writers claim that he ate locusts and honey and wore clothes made of camel hair.

A stained glass window depicting the baptism of Jesus Christ.

> ## The Trinity
>
> Christians believe in one God, but they also believe that God is three. This distinctive belief is called the **Trinity**. The three different 'persons' of the Trinity are called:
>
> * God the Father • God the Son • God the Holy Spirit.
>
> Christians believe that all three 'persons' of the Trinity are involved in Jesus's baptism. God the Father speaks from heaven, God the Son is baptised and God the Holy Spirit descends on Jesus like a dove.

❝ [1] Jesus returned from the Jordan full of the Holy Spirit and was led by the Spirit into the desert, [2] where he was tempted by the Devil for forty days. In all that time he ate nothing, so that he was hungry when it was over. ❞

❝ [3] The Devil said to him, 'If you are God's Son, order this stone to turn into bread.' ❞

❝ [4] But Jesus answered, 'The scripture says, "Human beings cannot live on bread alone."' ❞

❝ [5] Then the Devil took him up and showed him in a second all the kingdoms of the world. ❞

❝ [6] 'I will give you all this power and all this wealth,' the Devil told him 'It has all been handed over to me and I can give it to anyone I choose. [7] All this will be yours, then, if you worship me.' ❞

❝ [8] Jesus answered, 'The scripture says, "Worship the Lord your God and serve only him!"' ❞

> **9** Then the Devil took him to Jerusalem and set him on the highest point of the Temple, and said to him, 'If you are God's Son, throw yourself down from here. **10** For the scripture says, "God will order his angels to take good care of you." **11** It also says, "They will hold you up with their hands so that not even your feet will be hurt on the stones."

> **12** But Jesus answered, 'The scripture says, "Do not put the Lord your God to the test."'

> **13** When the Devil finished tempting Jesus in every way, he left him for a while.

Luke 4.1–13

Resisting temptation

In the Book of Genesis, the devil tempts Eve to eat an apple from the forbidden tree. In the story of Jesus's temptation, the devil uses food again, this time to tempt Jesus to prove he is the son of God. Jesus did not give in to the temptation, though. He told the devil that 'human beings cannot live on bread alone', meaning that humans need more than physical things to survive. Their spiritual life is also important, so he would continue fasting. The New Testament writers claim that Jesus lived a perfect, sinless life.

Next, the devil tried to test how faithful Jesus was to God. He told him to do something that would make him extremely popular among the Jews. The Jews thought their Messiah would lead them in battle against the Romans who were ruling over them, and that Israel would belong to the Jews again. The devil offered Jesus power over all the kingdoms of the world if he would bow down and worship him. Jesus refused. He quoted the first of the Ten Commandments to the devil: 'Worship the Lord your God and serve only him.'

The third temptation was a test of how much Jesus trusted God. The devil told him to perform a dramatic stunt of throwing himself from the top of the temple. The devil tried to persuade Jesus that the Jewish scriptures said God would send angels to catch him. If Jesus did this and was saved by God, it would show people that he was someone special. Once again, Jesus refused. This time, he quoted the fifth book of the Jewish scriptures, which says: 'Do not put the Lord your God to the test.'

After the devil's third attempt, he realised that Jesus was not going to be tricked or tempted, and so he left him alone.

Activity

Draw a table with three columns. In the first column, explain each of the three ways in which the devil tried to tempt Jesus. In the second column, state what Jesus said. In the third column, explain the meaning of Jesus's words.

Key vocabulary

baptism A ritual in which people are immersed in water to symbolise turning away from sin and following God

fast To eat very little or no food; at the time of Jesus, Jews often fasted as a way of helping them focus on God

ministry The name given to the three years that Jesus spent preaching and performing miracles

Trinity The belief that God is three as well as one – Father, Son and Holy Spirit

Check your understanding

1. Who was John the Baptist?
2. Why was Jesus's baptism unusual?
3. How did Jesus respond to the first temptation? What did he mean?
4. Why might the second and third temptations have been appealing to Jesus?
5. What do the baptism and temptations of Jesus show about his character?

Unit 3: New Testament: The life and teachings of Jesus
The miracles of Jesus

What miracles did Jesus perform and how did people react?

The Gospels record Jesus performing 35 miracles while he was on earth. Some of these miracles showed Jesus's power over nature – for example, calming storms and walking on water. He also used miracles to show his love for people by healing the sick and even bringing his friend Lazarus back to life after he died.

Traditionally, Christians believe that Jesus performed his first miracle at a wedding in a place called Cana. As the wedding moved into the night, the hosts ran out of wine. This would have been a cause of great embarrassment to them. When Jesus heard what had happened, he told the servants at the wedding to fill six large stone jars with water. Jesus turned the water into fine wine. This miracle is only recorded in John's Gospel.

> ### Fact
>
> Some Christians believe that the miracles described by the Gospel writers really happened. Others believe that the accounts of the miracles in the New Testament are not literally true but are intended to give a spiritual message or truth about God – for example, that he is loving or powerful.

The feeding of the 5000

The Gospels also tell how, on another occasion, Jesus was preaching in the countryside to a crowd of 5000 people. It grew late and the disciples told Jesus to let the crowds go into the surrounding villages to find food and somewhere to stay. Jesus told the disciples to ask people to sit down in groups of about 50. Jesus gathered the five loaves of bread and two fish that the disciples had and thanked God for them. The disciples passed the food around to the large crowd and miraculously there was enough for everyone to eat.

Jesus walks on water

After describing the feeding of the 5000, Matthew, Mark and John all tell a story about Jesus walking on water.

When the disciples first saw Jesus walking on the water, they did not recognise him and were terribly afraid.

Matthew writes that it was night-time, and the disciples were on a boat far out at sea, when Jesus started walking across the water towards them. The disciples were terrified and cried, 'It's a ghost!' Jesus told them not to be afraid. One of the disciples, Peter, asked Jesus if he could walk on the water with him. Peter walked on the water, but when a strong wind picked up he became fearful and began to sink. Jesus caught him and asked why he had lost his faith. The disciples were amazed by what they had seen. When Jesus got into the boat they worshipped him and said, 'Truly you are the Son of God.'

The healing of the paralysed man

66 ¹ A few days later Jesus went back to Capernaum, and the news spread that he was at home. ² So many people came together that there was no room left, not even out in front of the door. Jesus was preaching the message to them ³ when four men arrived, carrying a paralysed man to Jesus. ⁴ Because of the crowd, however, they could not get the man to him. So they made a hole in the roof right above the place where Jesus was. When they had made an opening, they let the man down, lying on his mat. ⁵ Seeing how much faith they had, Jesus said to the paralysed man, 'My son, your sins are forgiven.' 99

66 ⁶ Some teachers of the Law who were sitting there thought to themselves, ⁷ 'How does he dare talk like this? This is **blasphemy**! God is the only one who can forgive sins!' 99

66 ⁸ At once Jesus knew what they were thinking, so he said to them, 'Why do you think such things? ⁹ Is it easier to say to this paralysed man, "Your sins are forgiven," or to say, "Get up, pick up your mat, and walk"? ¹⁰ I will prove to you, then, that the Son of Man has authority on earth to forgive sins.' So he said to the paralysed man, ¹¹ 'I tell you, get up, pick up your mat, and go home!' 99

66 ¹² While they all watched, the man got up, picked up his mat, and hurried away. They were all completely amazed and praised God, saying, 'We have never seen anything like this!' 99

Mark 2.1–12

Jesus healing the paralysed man.

When the paralysed man came through the roof, nobody was expecting Jesus to tell him his sins were forgiven. They believed that only God could forgive sins, it was certainly not the job of a Jewish teacher. More to the point, the paralysed man had come to be healed, not have his sins forgiven, but Jesus wanted to show that he had the power to do both. The Jewish teachers of the Law were outraged that Jesus was claiming he could forgive sins. They thought he was committing **blasphemy**, because he was claiming to be equal to God.

Key vocabulary

blasphemy Disrespect towards God

Check your understanding

1 What was Jesus's first miracle?

2 How and why did Jesus feed 5000 people?

3 How did the disciples respond to Jesus walking on water?

4 Why did the 'teachers of the Law' get angry when Jesus healed the paralysed man?

5 Why might a Christian think that the miracles performed by Jesus in the Bible did not actually happen?

Unit 3: New Testament: The life and teachings of Jesus
Who were the Pharisees?

The Pharisees were a group of devout Jews, so why did Jesus come into conflict with them?

Before the time of Jesus, the Jews were expelled from the land that God had given them. They lived in Babylon and were ruled over by the Babylonians. They had no temple in which to worship, and some were worried that Jews would lose their identity and beliefs. To prevent this, a group of Jews called the **Pharisees** followed all 613 rules in the Torah very carefully. The Pharisees referred to themselves as the Chasidim, which means 'God's loyal ones'. They would not associate with non-Pharisees, because they believed that it could make them spiritually unclean.

The Pharisees and Jesus clashed repeatedly.

Why did Jesus clash with the Pharisees?

Jesus criticised the Pharisees because he thought that they were more concerned with following rules than following God. Jesus himself did not follow all their rules. For example, he healed people and picked food for his disciples on the Sabbath. The Pharisees carried out their spiritual activities publicly, as though to show everyone how religious they were. Jesus said that this was hypocritical and that the Pharisees cared more about what people thought of them than about truly honouring God. In addition, the Pharisees were often well-off, and Jesus was critical of their attitude to money as well as their unwillingness to associate with people who did not belong to their group.

The Sermon on the Mount

Matthew's Gospel includes a sermon delivered by Jesus, called the **Sermon on the Mount**. Much of what he said could be seen as criticism of the Pharisees.

> **Love your enemies**
> ❝ 43 You have heard that it was said, 'Love your friends, hate your enemies.' 44 But now I tell you: love your enemies and pray for those who persecute you,... 46 Why should God reward you if you love only the people who love you? Even the tax collectors do that! 47 And if you speak only to your friends, have you done anything out of the ordinary? Even the pagans do that! ❞
> Matthew 5.43–44, 46–47
>
> 6 ❝ 1 Make certain you do not perform your religious duties in public so that people will see what you do. If you do these things publicly, you will not have any reward from your Father in heaven. ❞

66 [2] So when you give something to a needy person, do not make a big show of it, as the hypocrites do in the houses of worship and on the streets. They do it so that people will praise them. I assure you, they have already been paid in full. [3] But when you help a needy person, do it in such a way that even your closest friend will not know about it. [4] Then it will be a private matter. And your Father, who sees what you do in private, will reward you. 99

Prayer

66 [5] When you pray, do not be like the hypocrites! They love to stand up and pray in the houses of worship and on the street corners, so that everyone will see them. I assure you, they have already been paid in full. [6] But when you pray, go to your room, close the door, and pray to your Father, who is unseen. And your Father, who sees what you do in private, will reward you. 99

Matthew 6.1–6

Fasting

66 [16] And when you fast, do not put on a sad face as the hypocrites do. They neglect their appearance so that everyone will see that they are fasting. I assure you, they have already been paid in full. [17] When you go without food, wash your face and comb your hair, [18] so that others cannot know that you are fasting – only your Father, who is unseen, will know. And your Father, who sees what you do in private, will reward you. 99

Money

66 [19] Do not store up riches for yourselves here on earth, where moths and rust destroy, and robbers break in and steal. [20] Instead, store up riches for yourselves in heaven, where moths and rust cannot destroy, and robbers cannot break in and steal. [21] For your heart will always be where your riches are... [24] You cannot be a slave of two masters; you will hate one and love the other; you will be loyal to one and despise the other. You cannot serve both God and money. 99

Matthew 6.16–21, 24

Jesus preaching the Sermon on the Mount.

Key vocabulary

Pharisees A group of Jews at the time of Jesus who followed the rules of the Torah very strictly

Sermon on the Mount A sermon given by Jesus giving guidance on how people should live their lives

Check your understanding

1. Who were the Pharisees?
2. Describe two things Jesus did that annoyed the Pharisees.
3. What did Jesus teach about loving enemies?
4. What did Jesus teach about money in the Sermon on the Mount?
5. How could Jesus be seen as criticising the Pharisees in the Sermon on the Mount?

The parable of the good Samaritan

Jesus often taught people using **parables**. Why did his radical messages cause controversy among his listeners?

Who were the Samaritans?

The Gospels tell how people often came to Jesus with questions about how they should live their lives. One day, a teacher of Jewish law approached Jesus wanting to know how to secure his place in heaven. He asked which people he should treat well and which people he could ignore or not care about.

Jesus answered the man's question with a parable. He said that there was once a Jewish man who was attacked on the road from Jerusalem to Jericho. This was a steep winding road, which made it easy for ambushers to hide. Jesus's audience would have known that it was a dangerous route that was popular among muggers.

In the parable, a man from Samaria is the only person who stops to help the injured man. People from Samaria were called **Samaritans**. They worshipped the same God as other Jews, but they had their own temple, and only followed the first five books of the Jewish scripture. Samaritans also believed it was acceptable to marry non-Jews. For these reasons, many other Jews at the time disliked the Samaritans.

The winding road from Jerusalem to Jericho.

Fact

At the time of Jesus, it was a traditional for priests to open the gates of the Temple after midnight for Passover. Samaritans did not worship with Jews, but, according to the Jewish historian Josephus, in around 9 CE some Samaritans secretly sneaked into Jerusalem and scattered human bones all around the Temple. This would have been seen as an act of great disrespect for the Jews, who viewed the Temple as the most holy place.

> 66 25 A teacher of the Law came up and tried to trap Jesus. 'Teacher,' he asked, 'what must I do to receive eternal life?' 99

> 66 26 Jesus answered him, 'What do the Scriptures say? How do you interpret them?' 99

> 66 27 The man answered, "'Love the Lord your God with all your heart, with all your soul, with all your strength, and with all your mind"; and "Love your neighbour as you love yourself.'" 99

> 66 28 'You are right,' Jesus replied; 'do this and you will live.' 99

> " ²⁹ But the teacher of the Law wanted to justify himself, so he asked Jesus, 'Who is my neighbour?' "

> " ³⁰Jesus answered, 'There was once a man who was going down from Jerusalem to Jericho when robbers attacked him, stripped him, and beat him up, leaving him half dead. "

> " ³¹ It so happened that a priest was going down that road; but when he saw the man, he walked on by on the other side. ³² In the same way a Levite also came there, went over and looked at the man, and then walked on by on the other side. ³³ But a Samaritan who was travelling that way came upon the man, and when he saw him, his heart was filled with pity. ³⁴ He went over to him, poured oil and wine on his wounds and bandaged them; then he put the man on his own animal and took him to an inn, where he took care of him. ³⁵ The next day he took out two silver coins and gave them to the innkeeper. '"Take care of him," he told the innkeeper, "and when I come back this way, I will pay you whatever else you spend on him."' "

> " ³⁶ And Jesus concluded, 'In your opinion, which one of these three acted like a neighbour toward the man attacked by the robbers?' "

> " ³⁷ The teacher of the Law answered, 'The one who was kind to him.' "

> " Jesus replied, 'You go, then, and do the same.' "

Luke 10.25–37

The good Samaritan carries the injured man to the inn.

What does the parable mean?

Through the parable of the good Samaritan, Jesus teaches that all people should be treated well, no matter who they are. This was a provocative message, because the Pharisees believed that they would become spiritually unclean by associating with non-Pharisees. Jesus's audience would have been shocked to hear a positive portrayal of a Samaritan – their traditional enemy. It might also have surprised them that the priest and the Levite were shown as being more concerned with rules and religion than with the wellbeing of other people.

Key vocabulary

parable A short story intended to make a particular point or give a moral lesson

Samaritans Jews from a region called Samaria, which lay on the border with northern Israel

Check your understanding

1. Why did other Jews look down on Samaritans?
2. Why did Jesus tell the parable of the good Samaritan?
3. What happened to the man travelling from Jerusalem to Jericho?
4. What did the Samaritan do in the parable?
5. Explain what Jesus's Jewish audience might have felt about the parable.

Unit 3: New Testament: The life and teachings of Jesus
The parable of the prodigal son

What happens in the parable of the **prodigal** son and how might Christians interpret it?

> 66 ¹¹ Jesus went on to say, 'There was once a man who had two sons. ¹² The younger one said to him, "Father, give me my share of the property now." So the man divided his property between his two sons. ¹³ After a few days the younger son sold his part of the property and left home with the money. He went to a country far away, where he wasted his money in reckless living. ¹⁴ He spent everything he had. Then a severe famine spread over that country, and he was left without a thing. ¹⁵ So he went to work for one of the citizens of that country, who sent him out to his farm to take care of the pigs. ¹⁶ He wished he could fill himself with the bean pods the pigs ate, but no one gave him anything to eat. 99

> 66 ¹⁷ 'At last he came to his senses and said, "All my father's hired workers have more than they can eat, and here I am about to starve! ¹⁸ I will get up and go to my father and say, 'Father, I have sinned against God and against you. ¹⁹ I am no longer fit to be called your son; treat me as one of your hired workers.'" 99

> 66 ²⁰ 'So he got up and started back to his father. He was still a long way from home when his father saw him; his heart was filled with pity, and he ran, threw his arms around his son, and kissed him. ²¹ "Father," the son said, "I have sinned against God and against you. I am no longer fit to be called your son." ²² But the father called to his servants. "Hurry!" he said. "Bring the best robe and put it on him. Put a ring on his finger and shoes on his feet. ²³ Then go and get the prize calf and kill it, and let us celebrate with a feast! ²⁴ For this son of mine was dead, but now he is alive; he was lost, but now he has been found."' And so the feasting began. 99

> 66 ²⁵ 'In the meantime the older son was out in the field. On his way back, when he came close to the house, he heard the music and dancing. ²⁶ So he called one of the servants and asked him, "What's going on?" ²⁷ "Your brother has come back home," the servant answered, "and your father has killed the prize calf, because he got him back safe and sound."' 99

> 66 ²⁸ 'The older brother was so angry that he would not go into the house; so his father came out and begged him to come in. ²⁹ But he answered his father, "Look, all these years I have worked for you like a slave, and I have never disobeyed your orders. What have you given me? Not even a goat for me to have a feast with my friends! ³⁰ But this son of yours wasted all your property, and when he comes back home, you kill the prize calf for him!" ³¹ "My son," the father answered, "you are always here with me, and everything I have is yours. ³² But we had to celebrate and be happy, because your brother was dead, but now he is alive; he was lost, but now he has been found."' 99

> Luke 15.11–32

The prodigal son working as a swineherd. Jews believe that pigs are unclean animals, so this job was the lowest type of work a Jewish person could do.

The forgiving father and angry elder brother

Christians believe that the father in this story represents God and the younger son represents sinners. They think the parable teaches that if people are genuinely sorry for their sins, God will forgive them and welcome them to his heavenly feast, no matter what they have done.

Luke often portrays the Pharisees negatively in his Gospel and the elder brother in this story is sometimes seen as representing the Pharisees. In the same way that the Pharisees were unhappy that Jesus spent time with sinners, the eldest son is angry with his father for throwing a party for his younger brother. The elder brother does not feel any joy that his brother has repented and returned home.

The father tells the elder brother that it is right to be happy and to celebrate this event. He points out that the eldest son had been so busy working to please him that he had not noticed how much he already had. He had also forgotten that his father already accepted him. This could be trying to make the point that the Pharisees should have felt joy when sinners repented. It could also be saying that the Pharisees were so busy trying to please God by following rules that they had forgotten that God already accepted them.

This parable teaches Christians that God is forgiving and that they too should forgive others when they are wronged. In the Gospels, Jesus teaches that people should always forgive, and never take revenge.

When his son returned, the father welcomed him with open arms, despite his sins.

Key vocabulary

prodigal Reckless or wasteful with money

Check your understanding

1 What does the younger son want at the start of the parable?
2 What happens to the younger son after leaving home?
3 How do the father and elder son respond to the younger son's return?
4 Who could the characters in the parable be seen as representing and why?
5 What might this parable teach Christians today?

Unit 3: New Testament: The life and teachings of Jesus
Outcasts, love and forgiveness

Why did Jesus's choice of companions concern groups such as the Pharisees?

Levi the disciple

Luke's Gospel tells how Jesus met a tax collector called Levi. Tax collectors were considered to be greedy and dishonest, but despite this Jesus asked Levi to become one of his disciples. Levi agreed and held a big feast in his house. The Pharisees complained: 'Why do you eat and drink with tax collectors and other **outcasts**?' However, Jesus felt that the sinners were the ones who really needed him. He explained to those who criticised him: 'People who are well do not need a doctor, but only those who are sick. I have not come to call respectable people to repent, but outcasts.'

A sinful woman crashes Simon's dinner

On another occasion, Jesus went for dinner at the house of a Pharisee called Simon. While he was there, a sinful woman came in and starting pouring perfume on Jesus's feet and washing, kissing and drying them with her hair. This was an extremely generous thing to do, because perfume was very expensive at this time.

Jesus calls Levi – also known as Matthew – to become one of his disciples.

Simon the Pharisee would not have been happy to have the woman in his house. He had probably invited Jesus for dinner to find out whether he was a prophet sent from God, and here Jesus was letting a sinful woman kiss and clean his feet. Simon decided that Jesus could not be sent from God; otherwise, he would not let this woman near him. But Jesus told the woman that her sins were forgiven because of her faith and the love that she had shown him. The Pharisees could not believe what they were seeing and hearing. Not only was Jesus spending time with sinners, but he was also praising them and forgiving them as if he were God.

Jesus believed that people should not judge others, and he warned against it in the Sermon on the Mount.

> 66 [1] Do not judge others, so that God will not judge you, [2] for God will judge you in the same way you judge others, and he will apply to you the same rules you apply to others. [3] Why, then, do you look at the speck in your brother's eye and pay no attention to the log in your own eye? [4] How dare you say to your brother, 'Please, let me take that speck out of your eye,' when you have a log in your own eye? [5] You hypocrite! First take the log out of your own eye, and then you will be able to see clearly to take the speck out of your brother's eye. 99
>
> Matthew 7.1–5

Love and forgiveness

Throughout Jesus's ministry, he taught that people should love others and love God. One of his most famous teachings is known as the Golden Rule: 'Do for others what you want them to do for you: this is the meaning of the Law of Moses and of the teachings of the prophets' (Matthew 7.12).

Once, when a Pharisee asked Jesus which commandment was the most important, Jesus answered: '"Love the Lord your God with all your heart, with all your soul, and with all your mind." This is the greatest and the most important commandment. The second most important commandment is like it: "Love your neighbour as you love yourself." The whole Law of Moses and the teachings of the prophets depend on these two commandments' (Matthew 22.37–40).

Jesus being thanked by one of the lepers he healed.

Jesus and the lepers

At the time of Jesus, lepers were outcasts. Lepers was a name given to people who had the skin disease leprosy, which was believed to be contagious. For this reason, people usually avoided lepers, but according to the Gospel writers Jesus healed lepers. In Luke's Gospel, he mentions Jesus healing 10 lepers at one time.

In the Sermon on the Mount, Jesus told his listeners that an important part of showing love is being kind and forgiving to others and not taking revenge.

> 66 38 You have heard that it was said, 'An eye for an eye, and a tooth for a tooth.' 39 But now I tell you: do not take revenge on someone who wrongs you. If anyone slaps you on the right cheek, let him slap your left cheek too. 40 And if someone takes you to court to sue you for your shirt, let him have your coat as well. 41 And if one of the occupation troops forces you to carry his pack one kilometre, carry it two kilometres. 42 When someone asks you for something, give it to him; when someone wants to borrow something, lend it to him. 99
>
> Matthew 5.38–42

Key vocabulary

outcasts People who are not accepted by society

Check your understanding

1. What is an outcast?
2. Why did Jesus's behaviour at Simon's house shock the Pharisees?
3. Why did Jesus warn against judging others in the Sermon on the Mount?
4. Explain what Jesus taught about loving other people.
5. 'Jesus's teachings are too difficult for people to follow.' Discuss this statement.

Unit 3: New Testament: The life and teachings of Jesus
Knowledge organiser

Key vocabulary

baptism A ritual in which people are immersed in water to symbolise turning away from sin and following God

Bethlehem The city where Jesus was born

blasphemy Disrespect towards God

disciples Jesus's 12 main followers

fast To eat very little or no food; at the time of Jesus, Jews often fasted as a way of helping them focus on God

Gospels The first four books of the New Testament; the word 'gospel' means 'good news'

incarnation God coming to earth as a human

ministry The name given to the three years that Jesus spent preaching and performing miracles

outcasts People who are not accepted by society

parable A short story intended to make a particular point or tell a moral lesson

Pharisees A group of Jews at the time of Jesus who followed the rules of the Torah very strictly

prodigal Wasteful

resurrection Coming back to life after dying

Samaritans Jews from the region called Samaria, which lay on the border with northern Israel

Sermon on the Mount A sermon given by Jesus giving guidance on how people should live their lives

Trinity The belief that God is three as well as one – Father, Son and Holy Spirit

Key facts

- The first four books in the New Testament are named after the people who may have written them: Matthew, Mark, Luke and John. Together, they are known as the Gospels. Each of these books is about a man called Jesus, who lived about 2000 years ago.

- Bible scholars think that most of the books in the New Testament were written within 70 years of Jesus's death, and some within 20 years.

- Matthew and Luke record the events of Jesus's birth, saying that he was born to Mary in Bethlehem, but there are also differences between their accounts.

- Luke says that at the age of about 30 Jesus was baptised by his cousin John and went into the wilderness, where he fasted for 40 days and nights and where the devil tried to tempt him in three ways.

- The Gospel writers record Jesus performing many miracles, including turning water to wine, the feeding of the 5000, walking on water and healing lepers and a paralysed man.

- The Gospels record Jesus coming into conflict with the Pharisees because he criticised their way of living, preferred to spend time with outcasts and claimed he could forgive sins, which they viewed as blasphemy.

- Jesus's teachings – for example, the Sermon on the Mount, the Golden Rule and parables including the prodigal son and good Samaritan – are recorded in the Gospels. Jesus taught that people should love God and love other people.

- Christians believe that Jesus was human, but they also believe he was God living on earth. They call God coming to earth as a human the incarnation. Christians believe in the Trinity.

John the Baptist baptises Jesus.

Key people

Herod The king who wanted Jesus to be killed as a baby

John the Baptist The man who baptised Jesus; sometimes said to be his cousin

Joseph The man engaged to Mary

Levi A tax collector who became a disciple of Jesus (also known as Matthew)

Mary The mother of Jesus

Peter Jesus's disciple who walked on water and denied knowing Jesus three times before the cockerel crowed

Simon the Pharisee A Pharisee who invited Jesus to dinner

The Sermon on the Mount.

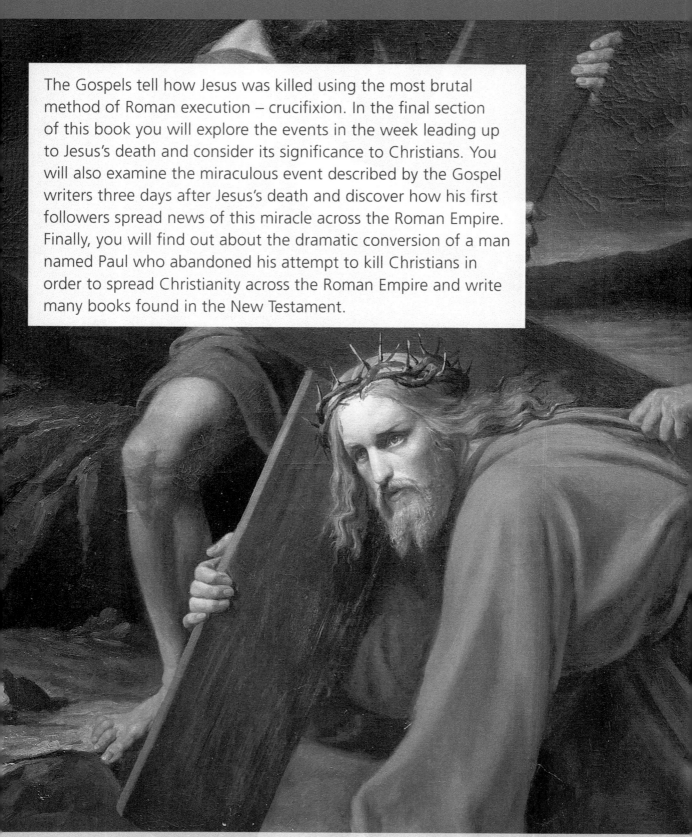

New Testament: Jesus in Jerusalem

The Gospels tell how Jesus was killed using the most brutal method of Roman execution – crucifixion. In the final section of this book you will explore the events in the week leading up to Jesus's death and consider its significance to Christians. You will also examine the miraculous event described by the Gospel writers three days after Jesus's death and discover how his first followers spread news of this miracle across the Roman Empire. Finally, you will find out about the dramatic conversion of a man named Paul who abandoned his attempt to kill Christians in order to spread Christianity across the Roman Empire and write many books found in the New Testament.

Unit 4: New Testament: Jesus in Jerusalem
The cleansing of the Temple

How did Jesus react when he saw the Temple being disrespected?

Having spent three years teaching and performing miracles, Jesus decided to go to Jerusalem. He entered the city riding a donkey. A **prophecy** in the Old Testament said that the Messiah would enter Jerusalem in this way. As Jesus entered, a large crowd gathered and praised him. Some people took off their cloaks and put them on the road. Others cut palm branches off the trees and spread them on the road. Palm leaves were a symbol of victory and triumph.

> 66 ⁹Rejoice, rejoice, people of Zion! Shout for joy, you people of Jerusalem! Look, your king is coming to you! He comes triumphant and victorious, but humble and riding on a donkey. 99
>
> Zechariah 9.9

Today, Christians celebrate Jesus's arrival in Jerusalem on Palm Sunday.

Jesus causes a scene

Jewish leaders were becoming increasingly concerned about the influence Jesus was gaining. The Gospels of Matthew, Mark and Luke record that, the day after arriving in Jerusalem, Jesus caused trouble in the Temple.

Jerusalem was very busy because it was the Jewish festival of Passover. Scholars estimate that there were around 2.5 million Jews in the city. People had travelled from many different areas and needed to change their money into local currency. Some dishonest men had set up their stalls in the Temple, where they were overcharging people. Others were using the Temple as a place to sell their animals. Jesus was infuriated by what he saw. In John, this story takes place earlier in Jesus's life than in Matthew, Mark and Luke. John also includes details not found in the other Gospels, and his interpretation of the events is different from those of the other Gospel writers.

Jesus goes to the Temple

66 ¹³It was almost time for the Passover Festival, so Jesus went to Jerusalem. ¹⁴There in the Temple he found people selling cattle, sheep, and pigeons, and also the moneychangers sitting at their tables. ¹⁵ So he made a whip from cords and drove all the animals out of the Temple, both the sheep and the cattle; he overturned the tables of the moneychangers and scattered their coins; ¹⁶and he ordered those who sold the pigeons, 'Take them out of here! Stop making my Father's house a marketplace!' ¹⁷His disciples remembered that the scripture says, 'My devotion to your house, O God, burns in me like a fire.' 99

66 ¹⁸ The Jewish authorities came back at him with a question, 'What miracle can you perform to show us that you have the right to do this?' 99

> 66 [19] Jesus answered, 'Tear down this Temple, and in three days I will build it again.' 99

> 66 [20] 'Are you going to build it again in three days?' they asked him. 'It has taken 46 years to build this Temple!' 99

> 66 [21] But the temple Jesus was speaking about was his body. [22] So when he was raised from death, his disciples remembered that he had said this, and they believed the scripture and what Jesus had said. 99
>
> John 2.13–21

The priests challenged Jesus, asking him what made him think he could behave in this way. John writes that Jesus replied by referring to his body as a temple. He told the priests that they would kill him, but that he would rise again three days later. The priests did not understand what he was talking about and were very confused. In describing this event, John quotes from a verse in the book of Psalms in the Old Testament: 'My devotion to your house, O God, burns in me like a fire.' He claims that the disciples understood this verse as referring to Jesus's actions. The other Gospel writers do not mention this. The story is known as the cleansing of the Temple, because Jesus cleansed the Temple of sinful behaviour.

Jesus driving the money-lenders from the Temple.

Key vocabulary

Palm Sunday The day Jesus entered Jerusalem on a donkey
prophecy A prediction that something will happen

Holy Week

Christians remember Jesus entering Jerusalem on **Palm Sunday**. It marks the start of a week that Christians call Holy Week. On the Monday, Christians remember Jesus going to the Temple. This is known as Holy Monday. The Thursday of Holy Week is known as Maundy Thursday and the Friday on which Jesus's death is remembered is Good Friday.

Check your understanding

1. What is the significance of Jesus entering Jerusalem on a donkey and of palm leaves?
2. What did Jesus do in the Temple and why?
3. How did the Jewish authorities respond to Jesus?
4. According to John, what did Jesus mean when he said 'tear down this Temple and I will rebuild it'?
5. Jesus is sometimes described as 'meek and mild'. Based on all you have learned so far, do you think this is a good description of his character?

Unit 4: New Testament: Jesus in Jerusalem
The Last Supper

What predictions did Jesus make during his final meal with his disciples?

What happened at the Last Supper?

Jesus attracted enormous crowds everywhere he went and Jewish leaders began to be afraid of the influence he had over people. They disliked how popular he was and felt that by comparing himself to God he was committing blasphemy. They wanted to be rid of him.

According to the first three Gospels, on the Thursday evening after Palm Sunday, Jesus and his disciples met at a friend's house in Jerusalem to share the Passover meal.

This meal is now known as the **Last Supper**. At the meal, Jesus broke some bread and shared it with the disciples, telling them that it was his body. He then gave them some wine and said it was his blood, poured out for many people. He told them to eat bread and drink wine in the future to remember him. The disciples had seen Jesus share bread and wine, but they had never heard him speak in this way before.

Leonardo da Vinci painted one of the most famous depictions of the Last Supper.

> ### Fact
>
> John records the meal of Jesus and his disciples happening earlier in the week. Unlike the other Gospel writers, he claims that during the meal Jesus got up and washed his disciples' feet. It was usual at this time for servants to wash the feet of guests, because the roads were dirty and dusty. Christians believe that by washing their feet Jesus was setting the disciples an example of how they should serve others.

Jesus's predictions

After eating, Jesus told his disciples that one of them would betray him to the authorities and that they would all abandon him. The disciples had given up everything to follow Jesus and were shocked that he would doubt their loyalty now. Peter told Jesus he would never abandon him, even if it meant dying with him. Jesus replied that before the cockerel crowed that night, Peter would deny knowing him three times.

After finishing their supper, the disciples and Jesus went to the **Garden of Gethsemane** to pray. Jesus was in great anguish – he knew what was about to happen. While in the garden, he told his disciples to keep watch while he prayed. According to the first three Gospels, Jesus prayed that, if possible, he would be spared from the suffering he was soon to go through. However, he also prayed to God: 'Not what I want, but what you want.' When Jesus went back to his disciples, he found them asleep. As he spoke to them, a crowd of men appeared, armed with weapons.

The arrest of Jesus

66 43 Jesus was still speaking when Judas, one of the twelve disciples, arrived. With him was a crowd armed with swords and clubs and sent by the chief priests, the teachers of the Law, and the elders. 44 The traitor had given the crowd a signal: 'The man I kiss is the one you want. Arrest him and take him away under guard.' 99

66 45 As soon as Judas arrived, he went up to Jesus and said, 'Teacher!' and kissed him. 46 So they arrested Jesus and held him tight. 47 But one of those standing there drew his sword and struck at the High Priest's slave, cutting off his ear. 48 Then Jesus spoke up and said to them, 'Did you have to come with swords and clubs to capture me, as though I were an outlaw? 49 Day after day I was with you teaching in the Temple, and you did not arrest me. But the Scriptures must come true.' 99

66 50 Then all the disciples left him and ran away. 99

66 51 A certain young man, dressed only in a linen cloth, was following Jesus. They tried to arrest him, 52 but he ran away naked, leaving the cloth behind. 99

Mark 14.43–52

Betrayed with a kiss

The crowd of men were led by Jesus's disciple Judas Iscariot. He had gone in secret to the Jewish priests and offered to help them arrest Jesus in exchange for 30 pieces of silver. Judas kissed Jesus so that the men would know which one of them he was. Jesus did not resist them when they arrested him. He said that this was what the scriptures had predicted would happen.

When they saw what was happening, the disciples were afraid that they would be attacked or arrested along with Jesus. As Jesus had predicted at the Last Supper, they fled, leaving Jesus alone. Later on, a girl recognised Peter as one of Jesus's followers, but Peter denied knowing him three times, just as Jesus had predicted.

Fact

According to Matthew, Judas felt guilty at betraying an innocent man, and so he threw the silver coins into the Temple and hanged himself. The author of Acts describes events differently, saying that Judas spent the money on a field, where he fell to his death. He burst open, causing all his insides to spill out.

Key vocabulary

Garden of Gethsemane The garden where Jesus was arrested

Last Supper Jesus's final meal with the disciples, where he predicts Peter's denial and Judas' betrayal

Check your understanding
1 Why did the Jewish authorities want to kill Jesus?
2 What was unusual about the way Jesus broke bread and shared wine?
3 What did Jesus correctly predict would happen?
4 What happened to Judas after he betrayed Jesus?
5 Why did Jesus not fight back when he was arrested?

Unit 4: New Testament: Jesus in Jerusalem
The plot against Jesus

Why did Pontius Pilate sentence Jesus to death?

Jesus on trial

After Jesus was arrested, he was taken to the Jewish leaders. They spat at Jesus, blindfolded him, punched him and mocked him, saying, 'tell us who hit you'. The Jewish leaders could not execute Jesus themselves because Jerusalem was part of the Roman Empire. Only the Roman governor, Pontius Pilate, could sentence Jesus to death.

Blaspheming against the Jewish God was not a crime under Roman law, so the Jews took Jesus to Pontius Pilate and accused him of breaking Roman laws. They claimed that Jesus was a troublemaker who was trying to stop the Jews being obedient to the Roman rulers. Because Jesus told people that he was King of the Jews, the Jewish leaders told Pilate that Jesus was guilty of **treason** – a crime that was punishable by death.

Pilate's problem

Pilate did not think that Jesus had committed any crime, but his political career depended on keeping peace in the area he governed. He did not want to anger the Jews, cause a riot or lose control of the city of Jerusalem. Passover was already a worrying time for the Romans, because it was a festival when the Jews remembered being freed from foreign rulers.

Pilate asked the crowd what he should do with Jesus.

With 2.5 million Jews in Jerusalem and 6000 soldiers on standby, Pilate did not want to risk any trouble breaking out in the city. As such, Pilate decided that he would give the crowd a choice to try and keep them happy. They could choose for him to free either Jesus or a murderer named Barabbas, who was also on trial. The crowd, who had probably been encouraged and assembled by the Jewish leaders, demanded that Barabbas was freed.

Pilate questions Jesus

❝ 11 Jesus stood before the Roman governor, who questioned him. 'Are you the king of the Jews?' he asked. ❞

❝ 'So you say,' answered Jesus. 12 But he said nothing in response to the accusations of the chief priests and elders. ❞

❝ 13 So Pilate said to him, 'Don't you hear all these things they accuse you of?' ❞

❝ 14 But Jesus refused to answer a single word, with the result that the governor was greatly surprised. ❞

Jesus is sentenced to death

66 15 At every Passover Festival the Roman governor was in the habit of setting free any one prisoner the crowd asked for. 16 At that time there was a well-known prisoner named Jesus Barabbas. 17 So when the crowd gathered, Pilate asked them, 'Which one do you want me to set free for you? Jesus Barabbas or Jesus called the Messiah?' 18 He knew very well that the Jewish authorities had handed Jesus over to him because they were jealous. 99

66 19 While Pilate was sitting in the judgment hall, his wife sent him a message: 'Have nothing to do with that innocent man, because in a dream last night I suffered much on account of him.' 99

66 20 The chief priests and the elders persuaded the crowd to ask Pilate to set Barabbas free and have Jesus put to death. 21 But Pilate asked the crowd, 'Which one of these two do you want me to set free for you?' 99

66 'Barabbas!' they answered. 99

66 22 'What, then, shall I do with Jesus called the Messiah?' Pilate asked them. 99

66 '**Crucify** him!' they all answered. 99

66 23 But Pilate asked, 'What crime has he committed?' 99

66 Then they started shouting at the top of their voices: 'Crucify him!' 99

66 24 When Pilate saw that it was no use to go on, but that a riot might break out, he took some water, washed his hands in front of the crowd, and said, 'I am not responsible for the death of this man! This is your doing!' 99

66 25 The whole crowd answered, 'Let the responsibility for his death fall on us and on our children!' 99

66 26 Then Pilate set Barabbas free for them; and after he had Jesus whipped, he handed him over to be crucified. 99

The soldiers mock Jesus

66 27 Then Pilate's soldiers took Jesus into the governor's palace, and the whole company gathered around him. 28 They stripped off his clothes and put a scarlet robe on him. 29 Then they made a crown out of thorny branches and placed it on his head, and put a stick in his right hand; then they knelt before him and mocked him. 'Long live the king of the Jews!' they said. 99

66 30 They spat on him, and took the stick and hit him over the head. 31 When they had finished making fun of him, they took the robe off and put his own clothes back on him. Then they led him out to crucify him. 99

Matthew 27.11–31

Key vocabulary

crucify To kill a person by tying or nailing to a large wooden cross

treason Plotting to betray or overthrow a ruler

Check your understanding

1 Why did the Jewish leaders have to persuade the Roman authorities to kill Jesus?

2 How did the Jewish leaders try to convince the Roman authorities?

3 What did Pilate do to try to keep the crowd happy?

4 How was Jesus treated by Pilate's soldiers?

5 Why did Pilate sentence Jesus to death?

The crucifixion of Jesus

How was Jesus killed?

Matthew records that Pontius Pilate handed Jesus over to his soldiers to be killed. First, they whipped him with a piece of leather containing metal and bone. Then they gave him a crown of thorns to wear and took him and the cross on which he would die to a place called Golgotha. They put a sign above him saying 'King of the Jews' to both mock him and warn others what would happen if they tried to stir up trouble against the Romans.

Jesus was forced to wear a crown of thorns to mock the idea that he was King of the Jews.

Jesus is crucified

❝ 25 It was nine o'clock in the morning when they crucified him. 26 The notice of the accusation against him said: 'The King of the Jews.' 27 They also crucified two bandits with Jesus, one on his right and the other on his left. ❞

❝ 29 People passing by shook their heads and hurled insults at Jesus: 'Aha! You were going to tear down the Temple and build it back up in three days! 30 Now come down from the cross and save yourself!' ❞

❝ 31 In the same way the chief priests and the teachers of the Law made fun of Jesus, saying to one another, 'He saved others, but he cannot save himself! 32 Let us see the Messiah, the king of Israel, come down from the cross now, and we will believe in him!' ❞

❝ And the two who were crucified with Jesus insulted him also. ❞

The death of Jesus

❝ 33 At noon the whole country was covered with darkness, which lasted for three hours. 34 At three o'clock Jesus cried out with a loud shout, 'Eloi, Eloi, lema sabachthani?' which means, 'My God, my God, why did you abandon me?' ❞

❝ 35 Some of the people there heard him and said, 'Listen, he is calling for Elijah!' 36 One of them ran up with a sponge, soaked it in cheap wine, and put it on the end of a stick. Then he held it up to Jesus's lips and said, 'Wait! Let us see if Elijah is coming to bring him down from the cross!' ❞

❝ 37 With a loud cry Jesus died. ❞

❝ 38 The curtain hanging in the Temple was torn in two, from top to bottom. 39 The army officer who was standing there in front of the cross saw how Jesus had died. 'This man was really the Son of God!' he said. ❞

Mark 15.25–39

The crucifixion in John and Luke

According to John, Pilate's soldiers broke the legs of the two criminals who were being crucified alongside Jesus, but because Jesus was dead they did not break his legs. Executioners would do this to speed up death – it stopped people using their thigh muscles to support their body weight. Instead of breaking Jesus's legs, they pierced his side with a spear, causing blood to flow out of his body.

The Gospel of John explains that, after Jesus died, Pilate gave his body to a follower of Jesus called Joseph of Arimathea. Joseph wrapped the body according to Jewish rituals and laid it in a tomb. A large stone was placed at the entrance. According to the Gospel of Matthew, Pontius Pilate sent a Roman soldier to guard the tomb, but John does not mention this.

Luke's Gospel says that while Jesus was on the cross he said: 'Father forgive them for they do not know what they are doing.' Luke also records a conversation between Jesus and one of the criminals hanging next to him.

How did crucifixion work?

In Roman times, crucifixion was used to kill the worst criminals. It was a brutal method of execution. The vertical post of a cross would usually be set in the ground, and condemned people would be led to the pole with their hands tied to the horizontal beam of wood. This was so that they could not resist. When they arrived at the vertical beam, their wrists would be nailed to the ends of the horizontal beam and then the horizontal beam would be lifted and attached to the vertical beam. Their feet were then nailed to the vertical beam.

Their death would be caused by the body's weight pulling downwards on the arms, making it increasingly hard to breathe. Due to the lack of oxygen in their blood, their heart and lungs stopped working properly and people died of suffocation. While on the cross, Jesus was offered wine mixed with a drug called myrrh to numb the pain. However, Jesus refused it.

Crucifixion was a slow and agonising way to die and was a form of execution that was only given to the worst criminals.

> 66 34 One of the soldiers, however, plunged his spear into Jesus's side, and at once blood and water poured out. (35 The one who saw this happen has spoken of it, so that you also may believe. What he said is true, and he knows that he speaks the truth.) 36 This was done to make the scripture come true: 'Not one of his bones will be broken.' 37 And there is another scripture that says, 'People will look at him whom they pierced.' 99
>
> John 19.34–37

> 66 39 One of the criminals hanging there hurled insults at him: 'Aren't you the Messiah? Save yourself and us!' 99

> 66 40 The other one, however, rebuked him, saying, 'Don't you fear God? You received the same sentence he did. 41 Ours, however, is only right, because we are getting what we deserve for what we did; but he has done no wrong.' 42 And he said to Jesus, 'Remember me, Jesus, when you come as King!' 99

> 66 43 Jesus said to him, 'I promise you that today you will be in Paradise with me.' 99
>
> Luke 23.39–43

Check your understanding

1 Why was a sign put above Jesus saying 'King of the Jews'?

2 How was Jesus mocked while he was on the cross?

3 How does John try to show that Jesus fulfilled prophecies in the Old Testament?

4 According to Luke's Gospel, what did Jesus and the criminal speak about on the cross?

5 Explain how crucifixion worked.

The resurrection of Jesus

What happened on the third day after Jesus's crucifixion?

Jesus died on a Friday. The next day, the Pharisees and other Jewish leaders went to Pontius Pilate, afraid that Jesus's body might be stolen...

> 66 [62] The next day, which was a Sabbath, the chief priests and the Pharisees met with Pilate [63] and said, 'Sir, we remember that while that liar was still alive he said, "I will be raised to life three days later." [64] Give orders, then, for his tomb to be carefully guarded until the third day, so that his disciples will not be able to go and steal the body, and then tell the people that he was raised from death. This last lie would be even worse than the first one.' 99
>
> 66 [65] 'Take a guard,' Pilate told them; 'go and make the tomb as secure as you can.' 99
>
> 66 [66] So they left and made the tomb secure by putting a seal on the stone and leaving the guard on watch. 99
>
> Matthew 27.62–66

Mary Magdalene sees Jesus resurrected

The four Gospels give different versions of what happened after Jesus's death, but each book claims that Jesus rose from the dead. According to John, early on the Sunday morning, a follower of Jesus called Mary Magdalene went to Jesus's tomb. When she arrived, she was shocked to find that the tombstone had been rolled away, and Jesus's body had vanished. She began to cry. Suddenly, two angels appeared where Jesus's body had been and asked her why she was weeping. She replied: 'They have taken my Lord away, and I do not know where they have put him.' Mary turned around and saw a man, who she thought was the gardener. He asked her: 'Why are you crying? Who is it that you are looking for?' Mary asked him if he had taken the body. As he replied, Mary saw that he was Jesus, risen from the dead.

Later that evening, Jesus appeared to all of his disciples except Thomas. When the disciples told Thomas they had seen Jesus, Thomas did not believe them. However, when he saw Jesus for himself, Thomas became convinced that Jesus was not simply a teacher, miracle worker or prophet, but was in fact God living on earth.

Jesus appears to his disciples

> 66 [19] It was late that Sunday evening, and the disciples were gathered together behind locked doors, because they were afraid of the Jewish authorities. Then Jesus came and stood among them. 'Peace be with you,' he said. [20] After saying this, he showed them his hands and his side. The disciples were filled with joy at seeing the Lord. [21] Jesus said to them again, 'Peace be with you.

As the Father sent me, so I send you.' ²² Then he breathed on them and said, 'Receive the Holy Spirit. ²³ If you forgive people's sins, they are forgiven; if you do not forgive them, they are not forgiven.' 99

Jesus and Thomas

66 ²⁴ One of the twelve disciples, Thomas (called the Twin), was not with them when Jesus came. ²⁵ So the other disciples told him, 'We have seen the Lord!' 99

66 Thomas said to them, 'Unless I see the scars of the nails in his hands and put my finger on those scars and my hand in his side, I will not believe.' 99

66 ²⁶ A week later the disciples were together again indoors, and Thomas was with them. The doors were locked, but Jesus came and stood among them and said, 'Peace be with you.' ²⁷ Then he said to Thomas, 'Put your finger here, and look at my hands; then reach out your hand and put it in my side. Stop your doubting, and believe!' 99

66 ²⁸ Thomas answered him, 'My Lord and my God!' 99

66 ²⁹ Jesus said to him, 'Do you believe because you see me? How happy are those who believe without seeing me!' 99

John 20.19–29

This painting by the Italian artist Caravaggio was painted around 1601. It shows Jesus guiding Thomas's hand into his wounds.

Acts

The fifth book of the New Testament is called Acts, which was written by the same person as Luke's Gospel. At the start of this book, Jesus is in Jerusalem with his disciples. He tells them that he is going back to heaven, but he will send them a 'comforter'. He tells them to wait in Jerusalem for this to happen. Jesus was talking about the Holy Spirit. He explains that the Holy Spirit will give the disciples the power to spread his message, not just in Jerusalem but throughout the whole world. After this, Jesus returns to heaven. His return to heaven is called the **ascension**.

66 ⁸ When the Holy Spirit comes upon you, you will be filled with power, and you will be witnesses for me in Jerusalem, in all of Judea and Samaria, and to the ends of the earth. 99

Acts 1.8

Key vocabulary

ascension Jesus's return to heaven after his resurrection

Fact

Christians disagree about whether Jesus physically rose from the dead or whether the accounts of his resurrection are myths. Christians who believe that the resurrection is a myth think that it communicates an important spiritual message that Jesus has power over death and those who follow him will have eternal life too.

Check your understanding

1 Why did the Pharisees and chief priests go to Pontius Pilate?

2 What happened to Mary Magdalene at Jesus's tomb?

3 What did Thomas want? What was his reaction when it happened?

4 How do different Christians interpret the resurrection accounts in the Gospels?

5 Explain what Jesus said would happen after his ascension.

Unit 4: New Testament: Jesus in Jerusalem
Why did Jesus die?

What do Christians believe about the death and resurrection of Jesus?

Explanations of why Jesus died can be placed into two categories. First, there are 'historical' explanations, which try to describe how the events in his life led to his crucifixion. Christians believe there are also theological– or religious – explanations for why Jesus died. These are based on the New Testament books that come after the Gospels. For Christians, the death of Jesus was not just a result of human events. It was part of God's plan to forgive people for their sins so they could be **reconciled** to him.

The Fall of humanity

Christians believe that God created humans to live in a perfect relationship with him. This perfect relationship was broken when Adam and Eve disobeyed God in the Garden of Eden (see pages 10–11). Their disobedience brought sin into the world.

God's plan

Christians believe that the Old Testament shows how God tried to repair his broken relationship with humanity. He tried to reconcile himself to humanity by choosing a nation of people, called the Israelites, to follow him. God wanted them to be a good example to all the other nations and lead them to worship of him. He gave the Israelites laws and spoke to them through the prophets. However, time and time again, they disobeyed and ignored God.

Christians believe that 2000 years ago God decided to fix his relationship with people by coming to earth as a human. They believe that Jesus's death was not just a result of him upsetting the Jews and Romans; they think it was God's plan for reconciling humanity to himself. Jesus came to earth to die for people's sins so that they could be forgiven and reconciled to God. Christians believe that God will always forgive people if they are genuinely sorry, no matter what they have done.

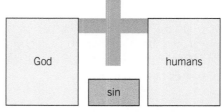

Christians believe that Jesus bridges the gap between humans and God that is caused by sin.

> 66 [3]God so loved the world that he gave his only son so that whoever believes in him will not perish but have eternal life. 99
>
> John 3.16

A final sacrifice for sin

When the Israelites sinned in the Old Testament, they sacrificed animals to God to ask for forgiveness. They would often put their hands on a lamb to symbolise passing their sins onto the lamb. The lamb would then be killed and its body would be burned. The Israelites believed that if people were truly sorry, then God would accept their sacrifices and forgive them.

In John's Gospel, John the Baptist describes Jesus as 'the lamb of God who takes away the sin of the world'. Christians believe that Jesus sacrificed his life for all people's sins. They believe that Jesus was the only person who could make this sacrifice for others, because, unlike all other humans, he was sinless. Christians believe that Jesus's sacrifice means that no more sacrifices need to be made.

> " [12] Sin came into the world through one man, and his sin brought death with it. As a result, death has spread to the whole human race because everyone has sinned... [18] So then, as the one sin condemned all people, in the same way the one righteous act sets all people free and gives them life. "
>
> Romans 5.12, 18

Because Jesus was resurrected three days after his death, Christians believe that he defeated death and made it possible for human souls also to survive death and go to heaven. Christians call Jesus their **saviour**, because he has saved them from sin and the punishment of sin, which is death.

The statue of Christ the Redeemer overlooks the Brazilian city of Rio de Janeiro. It took nine years to build and the statue's arms stretch 28 metres (92 feet) wide.

Activity

Create a spider diagram showing everyone who you think could be held responsible for Jesus's death. Include a reason for each. Put an H next to historical reasons and T next to theological reasons.

Key vocabulary

reconciliation When a broken relationship is restored

saviour Rescuer

Check your understanding

1. What do Christians believe broke humanity's perfect relationship with God?
2. According to Christians, how did God try to reconcile himself to humans in the Old Testament?
3. Why is Jesus's death and resurrection important to Christians?
4. Copy John 3.16 and the verses from Romans and explain what the verses mean.
5. Who was responsible for Jesus's death? Consider the role of the Jewish leaders, Pontius Pilate, the Roman soldiers, Judas and the disciples, Jesus, God, Adam and Eve.

Pentecost and the conversion of Saul

What life-changing experience happened to Saul on the road to Damascus?

Pentecost

According to Acts (the fifth book of the New Testament), after Jesus was resurrected from the dead, he ascended to heaven. Before his ascension, Jesus told the disciples to wait in Jerusalem for the Holy Spirit to come. About 50 days later, on a day called **Pentecost**, the disciples were together in a house. The Holy Spirit entered the house and filled the disciples, enabling them to speak in new languages. This experience transformed them.

When Jesus was arrested, his disciples abandoned him. However, seeing him alive again restored their faith. After they were filled with the Holy Spirit at Pentecost, they were even willing to be tortured and killed for spreading the message that Jesus had died and risen again to save people from their sins. The disciples performed miracles and preached about Jesus everywhere they went. On one occasion, after Peter preached to a huge crowd, 3000 people were baptised.

Persecution of the disciples

As more and more people believed the message that the disciples were spreading, the Jewish leaders became concerned. Peter and John were beaten and a follower of Jesus called Stephen was stoned to death for blasphemy. Stephen was the first of many Christians to become a **martyr**. His stoning was the start of widespread **persecution** of Christians. Many followers of Jesus escaped from Jerusalem, but a Pharisee called Saul was sent after them. Saul was passionate about Jewish traditions and hated what he considered to be the blasphemy of this new religion. However, one day, while travelling along a road to a place called Damascus, Saul had an experience that changed his life.

Saul on the road to Damascus.

The conversion of Saul

❝ [1] In the meantime Saul kept up his violent threats of murder against the followers of the Lord. He went to the High Priest [2] and asked for letters of introduction to the synagogues in Damascus, so that if he should find there any followers of the Way of the Lord, he would be able to arrest them, both men and women, and bring them back to Jerusalem. ❞

❝ [3] As Saul was coming near the city of Damascus, suddenly a light from the sky flashed around him. [4] He fell to the ground and heard a voice saying to him, 'Saul, Saul! Why do you persecute me?' ❞

❝ [5] 'Who are you, Lord?' he asked. ❞

Fact

Having two names was quite common in New Testament times. Saul is also called Paul in the Bible – Paul is his Roman name and Saul his Jewish one.

66 'I am Jesus, whom you persecute,' the voice said. 6 'But get up and go into the city, where you will be told what you must do.' 99

66 7 The men who were travelling with Saul had stopped, not saying a word; they heard the voice but could not see anyone 8 Saul got up from the ground and opened his eyes, but could not see a thing. So they took him by the hand and led him into Damascus. 9 For three days he was not able to see, and during that time he did not eat or drink anything. 99

66 10 There was a believer in Damascus named Ananias. He had a vision, in which the Lord said to him, 'Ananias!' 99

66 'Here I am, Lord,' he answered. 99

66 11 The Lord said to him, 'Get ready and go to Straight Street, and at the house of Judas ask for a man from Tarsus named Saul. He is praying, 12 and in a vision he has seen a man named Ananias come in and place his hands on him so that he might see again.' 99

66 13 Ananias answered, 'Lord, many people have told me about this man and about all the terrible things he has done to your people in Jerusalem. 14 And he has come to Damascus with authority from the chief priests to arrest all who worship you.' 99

66 15 The Lord said to him, 'Go, because I have chosen him to serve me, to make my name known to **Gentiles** and kings and to the people of Israel. 16 And I myself will show him all that he must suffer for my sake.' 99

66 17 So Ananias went, entered the house where Saul was, and placed his hands on him. 'Brother Saul,' he said, 'the Lord has sent me – Jesus himself, who appeared to you on the road as you were coming here. He sent me so that you might see again and be filled with the Holy Spirit.' 99

66 18 At once something like fish scales fell from Saul's eyes, and he was able to see again. He stood up and was baptised; 19 and after he had eaten, his strength came back. 99

Saul preaches in Damascus

66 Saul stayed for a few days with the believers in Damascus. 20 He went straight to the synagogues and began to preach that Jesus was the Son of God. 99

66 21 All who heard him were amazed and asked, 'Isn't he the one who in Jerusalem was killing those who worship that man Jesus? And didn't he come here for the very purpose of arresting those people and taking them back to the chief priests?' 99

Acts 9.1–21

Activity

Create a storyboard illustrating the story of Saul's **conversion** in eight still images. Include a caption for each image.

Key vocabulary

conversion Changing from one set of beliefs to another

gentiles A name given to non-Jews in the Bible

martyr Someone who dies for his or her beliefs

Pentecost The day on which the disciples were filled with the Holy Spirit

persecution Discrimination against a group of people

Check your understanding

1 What happened at Pentecost?
2 How did the experience on the day of Pentecost change the disciples?
3 What happened to people who became followers of Jesus?
4 Who was Saul? Why was he travelling to Damascus?
5 Explain what happened to Saul on the road to Damascus.

The travels and letters of Paul

What happened to Saul after his conversion?

Paul's mission

After his conversion, Paul was desperate to tell other Jews about Jesus. The Jewish leaders could not believe that Paul had converted to Christianity. While he was in Damascus, they tried to kill him. Damascus was surrounded by walls, so the only way out of the city was through the main gates. There were guards at the gates waiting to arrest Paul, but he managed to escape from the city by hiding in a basket and being lowered down through a hole in the wall!

Paul spent the rest of his life spreading the message about Jesus in the eastern parts of the Roman Empire. When they heard him preach, many Jews and gentiles believed his message and became Christians. These people formed Christian communities. Within 20 years of Jesus's death, most of the main towns near the Mediterranean Sea had a Christian community.

Not everybody was pleased to hear Paul's message. In some places, his preaching caused riots. He was stoned, whipped, thrown out of towns and often found himself put in prison for being a troublemaker. One time when Paul was in prison, there was a violent earthquake. All of the prisoners' doors flew open and they could escape. The jailer was so upset about what had happened that he grabbed his sword to kill himself. Paul stopped him, told him about Jesus and the jailer became a Christian.

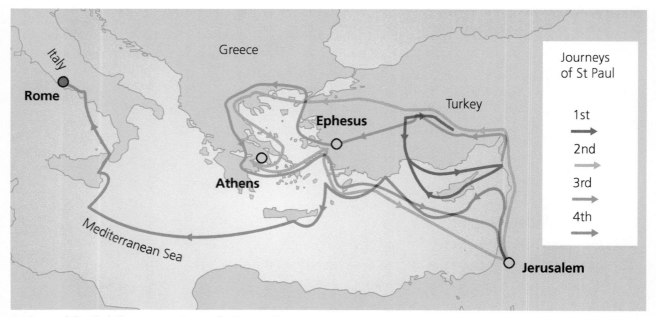

Paul spread the Christian message across the Roman Empire.

Paul's letters

Paul wrote letters to churches and Christians he had met on his travels. Thirteen of these letters are in the New Testament. The letters encourage the new Christians to keep their faith and give them instructions on how they should live and what they should believe.

Paul's letters are named after the people to whom they were written. For example, Galatians was written to Christians in Galatia and Colossians was written to Christians in Colossae. When Paul was writing these letters, he did not know that they would end up in a book called the Bible.

Biblical scholars disagree about whether Paul wrote all 13 books in the Bible that are credited to him. Some of them think that Paul's letters contradict each other and believe there are different styles between the letters, which suggests that others may have written under his name.

Paul's letters to the different churches in the Roman Empire are arranged in order of their length. The longest is Romans, so this comes first. The shortest is called 2 Thessalonians. After the letters to the churches, there are four other letters, which Paul wrote to his friends Timothy, Titus and Philemon. There are nine New Testament books after Paul's letters.

Books of the New Testament

The Gospels
Matthew
Mark
Luke
John

Acts (probably written by Luke)

Paul's letters to churches

Romans
1 Corinthians
2 Corinthians
Galatians
Ephesians
Philippians
Colossians
1 Thessalonians
2 Thessalonians

Paul's letters to friends

1 Timothy
2 Timothy
Titus
Philemon

Letters that were not written by Paul

Hebrews
James
1 Peter
2 Peter
1 John
2 John
3 John
Jude
Revelation

Check your understanding

1. Explain the problem facing Paul in Damascus.
2. Where did Paul spread his message and how did people respond to it?
3. Why did Paul write letters?
4. Why do biblical scholars disagree about whether Paul wrote all 13 letters credited to him?
5. How are Paul's letters named and how are they arranged in the New Testament?

Unit 4: New Testament: Jesus in Jerusalem
Knowledge organiser

Key facts

- In the week before his death, Jesus rode into Jerusalem on a donkey and was greeted by crowds who put down palm leaves. Christians remember this on Palm Sunday.

- The first three Gospel writers say that Jesus caused a disruption in the Temple in the week leading up to his death. This story is known as the 'cleansing of the Temple'. John places this story at an earlier point in Jesus's life.

- According to the first three Gospels, Jesus ate a meal with his disciples the night before he died. He told them to eat bread and drink wine in remembrance of him. He also predicted that he would be betrayed by the disciple Judas Iscariot and deserted by the other disciples.

- Jesus was arrested in the Garden of Gethsemane by the Jewish authorities. The Jewish leaders could not kill Jesus themselves because they were living under Roman rule, so they accused Jesus of treason to Pontius Pilate, who sentenced him to death.

- Jesus was mocked, tortured and killed by a brutal method of Roman execution called crucifixion. He died with a sign above him saying 'King of the Jews'. According to Luke, Jesus promised a criminal on a cross next to him that he would be in paradise with him that day.

- The Gospel writers claim that after Jesus's death he was resurrected, although their accounts of what happened after his death differ. Christians believe that the death and resurrection of Jesus made it possible for humans to be forgiven for their sins and be reconciled to God.

- The growth of the Christian Church after Jesus's death is recorded in the book of Acts. After being filled with the Holy Spirit on the day of Pentecost, the disciples spread the message about Jesus.

- A Pharisee named Saul/Paul originally persecuted Christians, but he converted to Christianity following a dramatic experience on the road to Damascus. He is credited with writing 13 of the books in the New Testament, although biblical scholars disagree about whether all 13 were actually written by him.

Key vocabulary

ascension Jesus's return to heaven after his resurrection

conversion Changing from one set of beliefs to another

crucify To kill a person by tying or nailing them to a large wooden cross

Garden of Gethsemane The garden where Jesus was arrested

gentiles A name given to non-Jews in the Bible

Last Supper Jesus's final meal with the disciples, where he predicts Peter's denial and Judas' betrayal

martyr Someone who dies for their beliefs

Palm Sunday The day Jesus entered Jerusalem on a donkey

Pentecost The day that the disciples were filled with the Holy Spirit

persecution Discrimination against a group of people

prophecy A prediction that something will happen

reconciliation When a broken relationship is restored

saviour Rescuer

treason Plotting to betray or overthrow a ruler

Leonardo da Vinci painting of the Last Supper.

Key people

Barabbas A murderer who was due to be executed, but whom the crowd chose to set free instead of Jesus

Judas Iscariot The disciple who betrayed Jesus in exchange for 30 pieces of silver

Mary Magdalene A follower of Jesus who was the first person to see him after his resurrection

Pontius Pilate The Roman governor who sentenced Jesus to death

Saul/Paul A Pharisee who persecuted Christians until his conversion to Christianity on the road to Damascus; he is credited with writing 13 letters found in the New Testament

Thomas A disciple who doubted Jesus's resurrection until he saw Jesus's wounds for himself

Index

Acknowledgements

Every effort has been made to trace copyright holders and to obtain their permission for the use of copyright material.

The publishers will gladly receive any information enabling them to rectify any error or omission at the first opportunity.

The publishers would like to thank the following for permission to reproduce copyright material:

(t = top, b = bottom, c = centre, l = left, r = right)

Text

Good News Bible © 1994 published by the Bible Societies/HarperCollins*Publishers* Ltd UK, used with permission.

Photographs

Cover and title page ASP Religion/Alamy Stock Photo, pp6–7 Brian Jackson/Alamy Stock Photo, p8 t Tyler Panian/Shutterstock, p8 c GL Archive/Alamy Stock Photo, p8 b Polyanska Lyubov/Shutterstock, p10 FineArt/Alamy Stock Photo, p11 Chronicle/Alamy Stock Photo, p12 jorisvo/Shutterstock, p13 robertharding/Alamy Stock Photo, p14 Lebrecht Music& Arts Photo Library/Alamy Stock Photo, p15 Chronicle/Alamy Stock Photo, p16 t Archivart/Alamy Stock Photo, p16 b Carmen Medlin/Shutterstock, p19 t Prisma Archivo/Alamy Stock Photo, p19 b jozef sedmak/Alamy Stock Photo, p20 Everett-Art/ Shutterstock, p21 Mary Evans Picture Library/Alamy Stock Photo, p22 Heritage Image Partnership Ltd/ Alamy Stock Photo, p23 Granger Historical Picture Archive/Alamy Stock Photo, p24 jorisvo/Shutterstock, p25 robertharding/Alamy Stock Photo, pp26–27 prisma Archivo/Alamy Stock Photo, p29 l jorisvo/ Shutterstock, p29 r Lebrecht Music& Arts Photo Library/Alamy Stock Photo, p30 Art Directors&Trip/ Alamy Stock Photo, p31 Vito Arcomano/Alamy Stock Photo, p33 t heritage Image Partnership Ltd/Alamy Stock Photo, p33 b Prisma Archivo/Alamy Stock Photo, p34 George Muresan/Shutterstock, p37 t Nicku/ Shutterstock, p37 b World History Archive/Alamy Stock Photo, p39 t GL Archive/Alamy Stock Photo, p39 b Asier Villafranca/Shutterstock, p41 t SuperStock/Alamy Stock Photo, p41 b lebrecht Music& Arts Photo Library/Alamy Stock Photo, p42 Art Directors&Trip/Alamy Stock Photo, p43 505 collection/Alamy Stock Photo, p45 t jorisvo/Shutterstock, p45 b Mary Evans Picture Library/Alamy Stock Photo, pp46–47 The Print Collector/Alamy Stock Photo, p48 t Lane V. Erickson/Shutterstock, p48 b Steve Skjold/Alamy Stock Photo, p50 chronicle/Alamy Stock Photo, p51 Sabino Parente/Shutterstock, p52 ASP Religion/Alamy Stock Photo, p54 Nicku/Shutterstock, p55 Renata Sedmakova/Shutterstock, p56 renata Sedmakova/ Shutterstock, p57 Niday Picture Library/Alamy Stock Photo, p58 www.BibleLandPictures.com/Alamy Stock Photo, p59 Freedom Studio/Shutterstock, p60 Artokoloro Quint Lox Limited/Alamy Stock Photo, p61 Art Reserve/Alamy Stock Photo, p62 lebrecht Music& Arts Photo Library/Alamy Stock Photo, p63 lebrecht Music& Arts Photo Library/Alamy Stock Photo, p65 t mary Evans Picture Library/Alamy Stock Photo, p65 b Renata Sedmakova/Shutterstock, pp66–67 jozef sedmak/Alamy Stock Photo, p68 North Wind Picture Archives/Alamy Stock Photo, p69 IanDagnall Computing/Alamy Stock Photo, p70 t Renata Sedmakova/Shutterstock, p70 b INTERFOTO/Alamy Stock Photo, p72 Lebrecht Music& Arts Photo Library/Alamy Stock Photo, p74 Michael Flippo/Alamy Stock Photo, p75 Jan Wachala/Alamy Stock Photo, p77 Artepics/Alamy Stock Photo, p79 Mark Schwettmann/Shutterstock, p80 chronicle/Alamy Stock Photo, p85 Renata Sedmakova/Shutterstock.